ignite English

Teacher Companion

Christopher Edge
Liz Hanton
Mel Peeling
Martin Phillips
Alison Smith

Consultant
Geoff Barton

OXFORD
UNIVERSITY PRESS

OXFORD
UNIVERSITY PRESS

Great Clarendon Street, Oxford, OX2 6DP, United Kingdom

Oxford University Press is a department of the University of Oxford.
It furthers the University's objective of excellence in research, scholarship, and education
by publishing worldwide. Oxford is a registered trade mark of Oxford University Press in
the UK and in certain other countries

British Library Cataloguing in Publication Data

Data available

978-0-19-839246-0

10 9 8 7 6 5 4 3 2 1

Paper used in the production of this book is a natural, recyclable product made from
wood grown in sustainable forests. The manufacturing process conforms to the
environmental regulations of the country of origin.

Printed in Great Britain by Bell and Bain Ltd., Glasgow

Links to third party websites are provided by Oxford in good faith and for information
only. Oxford disclaims any responsibility for the materials contained in any third party
website referenced in this work.

Page layout by Phoenix Photosetting.

Contents

Ignite English has been written by people who love teaching English. It was a pre-requisite for us when developing this resource that you have people who are confident teaching English and who would find it patronizing to tell you how to teach English. Therefore we have provided a flexibility, both digitally and on the page, so that you can decide how you are going to customize it for your students.

In *Ignite English*, we also take English and show how it relates to the real world. Outside school there are lots of people doing lots of different jobs who will be using speaking, listening, reading and writing, and we might not even think about how they are doing it. Well let's! In *Ignite English*, we take a look at what they do and we talk to them about how they are doing it, so that you and your students can explore the way they are using language and connect what we are doing in the classroom with the world out there.

Informed by research and recent Ofsted reports, *Ignite English* aims to help reinvigorate KS3 English teaching and learning by:

- Improving learning through relevance and creativity
- Ensuring teaching is distinctive
- Enabling effective transition between Year 6 and Year 7
- Accessing up-to-date and relevant professional development
- Delivering the new KS3 National Curriculum

That is essentially what we are trying to do with *Ignite English*.

Geoff Barton

Series Consultant, Head Teacher, Teacher of English and highly experienced English author

Ignite English authors

Ignite English was created with Geoff Barton and authored by experienced teachers and educationalists who are passionate about teaching English. As well as being tested in schools and reviewed by teachers, the resources were also reviewed by Peter Ellison, a cross-phase Local Authority Adviser and Phil Jarrett, former Ofsted National Adviser for English.

Relevance

English as a subject covers all sorts of reading, writing and spoken English skills, texts and contexts. Our intention is to help students see the connections between what they are learning in English lessons in school and the world beyond the school gate.

So, in *Ignite English*, students will meet a range of people, from writers and actors through to business people and the military, whose jobs are linked thematically to the unit they are exploring. Many of the reading, writing and spoken English skills that students need every day are the skills they need to develop through their English lessons. *Ignite English* also aims to help students understand how they can apply the key English skills they are developing in real-world contexts.

Creativity

Being able to respond in a creative and personal way is a vital part of English lessons. *Ignite English* offers students a wide range of reading, writing and spoken English tasks that ask students to respond in lots of different and creative ways. From tweeting and texting to selecting winning texts for a competition to essays and reports, *Ignite English* aims to provide students with variety and opportunities for creativity.

Distinctiveness

Learning what students are good at and learning what they need to improve on are an essential part of English.

Each unit in *Ignite English* opens with a 'big question', which sits underneath all the learning that will happen throughout that unit. At appropriate points in each unit, students have opportunities to evaluate their progress and at the end of the unit they will have an assessment, often in a real-world context, which gives them the opportunity to show what they have learned.

All of these features aim to allow students to understand more about the texts and skills offered in English lessons, to discover what interests them and to express themselves clearly in relevant, creative and distinctive ways.

Transition support

Teacher Companion 1 includes English lesson suggestions and guidance on effective transition from Primary to Secondary school. It also includes a range of teaching ideas for the first week of English lessons in Secondary schools, with an opening lesson included in Student Book 1. In addition, there is a professional development unit specifically on transition in Kerboodle: Lessons, Resources and Assessment.

Also on Kerboodle LRA 1 and on the Oxford University Press *Ignite English* webpage, you will find a unit of work, with transition tips, for Primary school teachers to use in the final term of Year 6. This unit, 'Making a Difference', has *Ignite English* principles at its heart and we hope that by passing this unit on to local Primary schools it will foster enhanced relationships between Secondary school English departments and colleagues in local Primary schools.

Student Books

The Student Books have been designed to develop a range of reading, writing and spoken English skills in real life contexts. Each Student Book offers thematically-focused units, covering prose fiction, poetry, drama and non-fiction forms, as well as a focus on language and one unique immersive unit based around a real-world scenario. They also feature an explicit focus on spelling, punctuation and grammar (SPAG). There is a wide range of source texts and activities with Stretch and Support as well as regular Progress Checks and Extra Time features, which can be used either for extension or homework.

Teacher Companions

Each Teacher Companion shares the thinking and philosophy behind the resources with a focus on the 'why', 'what' and 'how' of each unit, lesson and assessment. Additionally, the Teacher Companions feature unit-by-unit teaching support materials with comprehensive teaching tips, links and further reading suggestions. Each lesson features a Lesson Companion that includes a range of teaching ideas, guidance and tips to enable you to customize your lessons. The Teacher Companion also includes guidance and suggestions on setting up and marking the end-of-unit assessments.

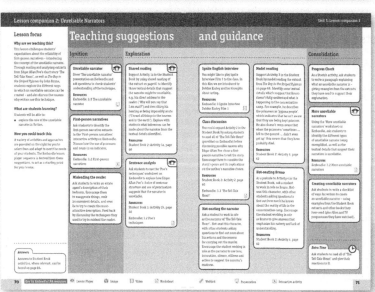

Kerboodle: Lessons, Resources and Assessment

Kerboodle is packed full of guided support and ideas for creating and running effective lessons. It's intuitive to use, customizable, and can be accessed online anytime and anywhere. *Ignite English* Kerboodle LRA includes:

- 18 exclusive interviews providing over 40 unique and compelling films, connecting the learning in KS3 English lessons to skills used in thematically-linked jobs

- Eight specially-commissioned filmed units providing CPD for English departments on key areas of Key Stage 3 teaching and learning, including genuine lesson footage, interviews with Primary and Secondary school teachers and students, and comments and observations from Geoff Barton and Phil Jarrett

- Materials to support the transition for students from Key Stage 2 to Key Stage 3

- Grammar support for teachers and students through extensive spelling, punctuation and grammar interactives and a grammar reference guide

- A wealth of additional resources including: interactive activities, an editable alternative end-of-unit assessment for every Student Book unit, marking scales to help monitor progress, photos, editable presentations, editable worksheets (general, differentiation and peer/self-assessment) and weblinks

- Lesson Player, enabling teachers to deliver ready-made lessons or the freedom to customize plans to suit your classes' needs

Kate Geary and Matthew Grainger, Oxfam:

'Simplify the message.'

Kerboodle Online Student Books

All three student books are also available as Online Student Books. These can be accessed on a range of devices, such as tablets, and offer a bank of tools to enable students to personalize their book and view notes left by the teacher.

Ignite English Kerboodle: Lessons, Resources and Assessment is packed full of guided support and ideas for running and creating effective KS3 English lessons. It's intuitive to use, customizable, and can be accessed online. It also includes teacher access to the accompanying *Ignite English* Kerboodle Book.

Ignite English Kerboodle: Lessons, Resources and Assessment provides hundreds of lively built-in resources, including unique specially commissioned films, interactive activities, ready-to-go lesson presentations, and supported assessment tasks with marking guidance. You can adapt many of these resources to suit you and your students' individual needs and upload your existing resources so everything can be accessed from one location.

Lessons

Ready-to-play lesson presentations (Lesson Player) complement every lesson in the book. Each Lesson Player is easy to launch, and features a ready-made lesson derived from the Ignition, Exploration and Consolidation activities in the corresponding Lesson Companion found in the Teacher Companion. These ready-made lessons include: unit objectives, an Ignition activity, Exploration activities and a Consolidation activity plus all the relevant resources (such as **Ignite Interview** films, worksheets, images, interactive activities and presentations).

You can further personalize the lessons by adding in your own resources and notes or bringing in other resources from elsewhere in *Ignite English*. Your lessons and notes can be accessed by your whole department – they are a great time-saver and ideal for non-specialist teachers and cover lessons.

> The Lessons module contains ready-to-play lesson plans and presentations that complement every lesson in the *Ignite English* Student Book

> Resources are built into each Lesson Player so all the relevant activities, films and worksheets are ready to launch

> For each lesson, a printable set of teacher notes are also available as a guide to support your lesson delivery, and provide further ideas or tips that only teachers can see

> The resources you want to use can also be rearranged and launched in sequence to suit your classroom needs

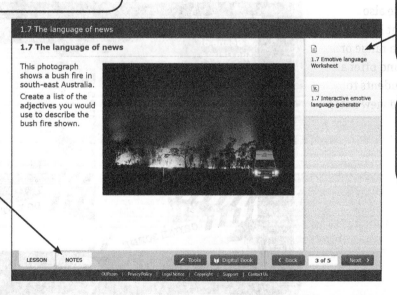

Ignite English Lesson Player

Resources

Ignite English Kerboodle: Lessons, Resources and Assessment has a wealth of resources for teachers and students. In **Kerboodle**, to access the full list of resources for *Ignite English*, click on the **Resources tab** at the top of the screen.

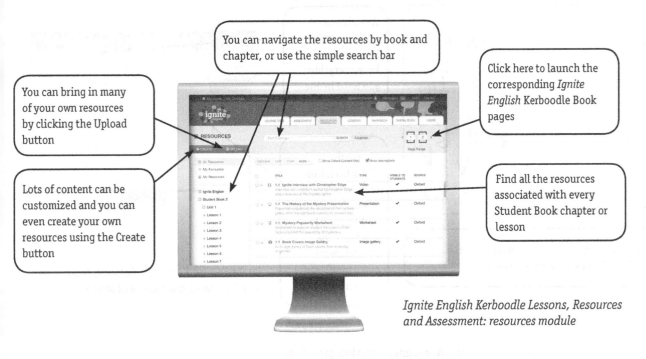

You can navigate the resources by book and chapter, or use the simple search bar

Click here to launch the corresponding *Ignite English* Kerboodle Book pages

You can bring in many of your own resources by clicking the Upload button

Lots of content can be customized and you can even create your own resources using the Create button

Find all the resources associated with every Student Book chapter or lesson

Ignite English Kerboodle Lessons, Resources and Assessment: resources module

Kerboodle resources are fully integrated with the *Ignite English* Student Books and Teacher Companions.

The resources module is packed full of Ignite Interview film clips, images, presentations, interactive activities and worksheets

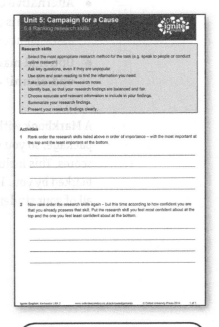

Worksheet on research skills from Kerboodle LRA 2, Unit 5: Campaign for a Cause

Assessment and Markbook

Click on the **Assessment tab** to find the assessment materials to help you deliver a varied and effective assessment programme.

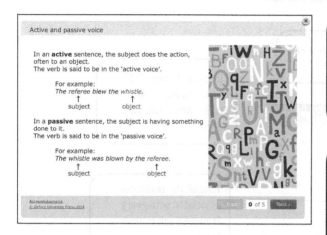

A markbook and a reporting function help keep everything you need in one place

Alternative editable end-of-unit assessments available for every unit to provide a wider range of assessment opportunities in different modes

Ignite English Kerboodle Lessons, Resources and Assessment: assessment module

A bank of assignable spelling, punctuation and grammar interactives include automarking to save time

The Assessment section provides:

- **SPAG interactives:** A bank of assignable spelling, punctuation and grammar interactive activities to help improve students' technical accuracy. Automarked interactives have marks automatically reported in the **Markbook**.

- **Alternative end-of-unit assessments:** Alternative editable end-of-unit assessments available for every Student Book unit to provide a wider range of assessment opportunities in different modes

- **Optional marking scales for use with reading, writing and spoken English end-of-unit assessments:** To help monitor progress

A **Markbook** with reporting functionality completes the Kerboodle assessment package, so you can keep track of all your students' test results and assessment scores. This includes both the auto-marked tests and work that needs to be marked by you. It is also easy to import class registers and create user accounts for all of your students.

Ignite English Kerboodle Book

Ignite English Kerboodle Book provides you with an on-screen version of the Student Book for use on your whiteboard with the whole class.

Teacher access to the *Ignite English* Kerboodle Book is **automatically available** as part of the Lessons, Resources and Assessment package. You can also choose to buy access for your students.

Both teacher and student access include a simple **bank of tools** so you can personalize the book and make notes.

It can be accessed on other devices, such as tablets.

You and your students can use different tools such as Sticky Notes, Bookmarks and Pencil features to personalize each page

You can Zoom in and Spotlight any part of the text

Every teacher and student has their own digital notebook for use within their Kerboodle Book

You can quickly navigate around the book with the contents menu or page number search

Unit overview

The chapters in this Teacher Companion link directly to the corresponding Student Book theme, but also aim to provide you with holistic thematic and practical support, both for planning and lesson delivery purposes. This starts with looking at the 'why', 'what' and 'how' for the unit as a whole, and then providing a snapshot medium-term outline. All of the subsequent ideas and guidance reflect the underpinning philosophy of *Ignite English*, allowing you the flexibility to adapt all the materials to suit the needs of your students, your department and your teaching style.

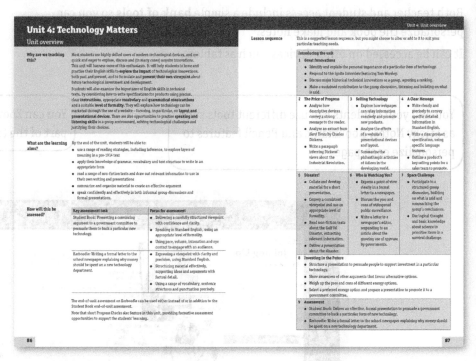

Preparing to teach

The preparing to teach sections in each chapter aim to equip you with useful background to the theme, saving you time but also enabling you to feel more confident when delivering the unit. Weblinks and wider reading, both for you and your students, is also included. Comprehensive practical teaching tips, in the context of the specific unit, conclude the preparing to teach section.

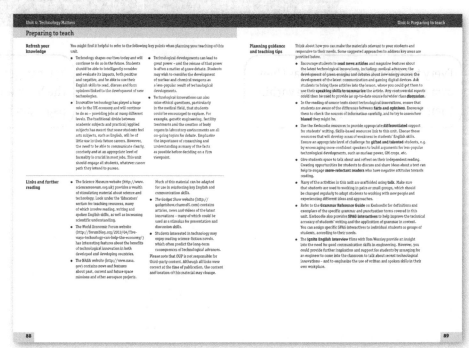

Lesson Companions

Each 'lesson' in the Student Book has a corresponding Lesson Companion in this Teacher Companion. The Lesson Companions open with sharing the 'why', 'what' and 'how' for each specific lesson. The main aim of each Lesson Companion is to provide you with a number of teaching ideas and tips, some of which relate to resources provided on the Kerboodle LRA, others are standalone. Guidance is also provided on Student Book activities. The intention is that from these lesson ideas you can create your own lessons, putting a selection of the ideas into a sequence or using some in parallel with different groups of students or individual students in your class. The Ignition, Exploration and Consolidation headings are a guide only – individual lesson ideas can be used in the way that suits your needs best. If you would like to follow a suggested route through the lesson ideas, these are indicated with the ⌂ symbol, and relate to the lesson sequence as it appears in the Kerboodle LRA Lesson Player.

The Lesson Companions also include guidance on the Extra Time Student Book features, which can be used either in class or as homework tasks. Additional Extra Time activities have been added to the Lesson Companions.

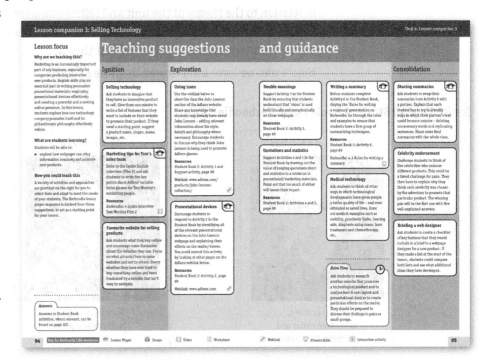

Assessment guidance and answers

Suggestions on how to set up and run the end-of-unit assessments is provided at the end of each chapter, together with guidance on marking. Answers to Student Book activities, where appropriate, are provided on the final page of each Teacher Companion chapter.

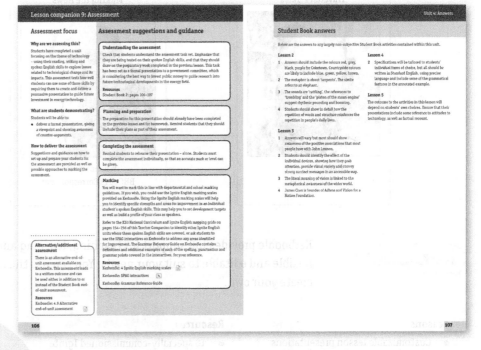

Ignite English features 18 specially-commissioned interviews, comprising over 40 films on Kerboodle: Lessons, Resources and Assessment. Introductions and quotations from the interviewees also appear throughout the Student Books.

These interviews, which are thematically linked to each Student Book unit, provide a direct connection for students with the relevant reading, writing or spoken English skills that they are developing in *Ignite English* and in English lessons generally.

The first film in every unit, and the introduction to every unit in the Student Books, provides an introduction to the interviewee, background to what they do in relation to the theme of the unit and initial comments on the skills they use. Subsequent films provide more specific skills comments and wider information about the interviewee and the work that they do.

Here's who we have interviewed in *Ignite English*:

Ignite English Student Book 1 and Kerboodle LRA 1

In Search of Adventure

Mick Conefrey,
Adventure writer and
documentary maker

The Identity Kit

Dreadlock Alien,
Performance poet

Out of This World

Jaine Fenn,
Science-fiction author

Travellers' Tales

Hugh Thomson,
Travel writer

Making the News

Will Gompertz,
BBC Arts Correspondent

Your Language

Maeve Diamond,
Accent and dialect coach

Kerboodle provides full support for teaching, learning and assessment but is also flexible and editable to suit your needs. You can use the lessons provided, or create your own.

Lessons
- Customizable lesson presentations and plans with resources launched directly from the presentation
- Teacher notes accompany every lesson
- Editable planning documents

Resources
- 18 specially-commissioned Ignite Interviews
- A wealth of photos, worksheets, presentations and interactive activities
- 8 specially-commissioned film-based CPD units
- Year 6 to Year 7 transition materials
- A comprehensive grammar guide

Assessment
- Alternative end-of-unit editable assessments
- A bank of assignable spelling, punctuation and grammar interactive activities
- Optional marking scales to help monitor progress
- Online markbook

Ignite English **Student Book 2 and Kerboodle LRA 2**

It's a Mystery

Christopher Edge,
Mystery writer

Words of War

Ed Boanas,
Infantry officer

Appearance and Reality

Debbie Korley,
Actress

Technology Matters

Tom Worsley,
Engineer

Campaign for a Cause

Kate Geary and Matthew Grainger,
Media and Communications at
Oxfam

Power of Communication

Dominic Gettins,
Advertising agency: Head of
writing

Ignite English **Student Book 3 and Kerboodle LRA 3**

Dare to Scare

Sarah Pinborough,
Horror writer

Relationships

Nick Cope,
Song-writer and musician

Exploring Difference

Nikki Emerson,
Wheelchair track athlete

My Life, My Choices

Lisa Sewards,
Feature writer

Young Entrepreneurs

Renée Watson,
Business owner

From Talking Drums to Tweets

Fiona McPherson,
Oxford English Dictionary editor

Unit 1: It's a Mystery

Unit overview

Why are we teaching this?

With their intrigue and drama, mysteries have a unique power to **engage students' imaginations**. The mystery genre is also one that students often choose to **read for pleasure**, so it can provide a motivating route into the study of classic literary texts, such as 'The Adventure of the Speckled Band'.

Students are able to participate actively in mystery fiction – using reading, speaking and listening, and critical-thinking skills to solve the mystery themselves before the solution is revealed. The genre provides a purposeful context for teaching skills, such as **close reading**, **inference** and **deduction**. The unit also provides a context for exploring **plot structure**, **characterization**, **setting** and **narrative viewpoint**, as well as the **vocabulary** and **grammatical features** of writing mystery fiction. Students move from exploring the **conventions of the genre** in the texts they read, to demonstrating their understanding by writing their own short mystery story.

What are the learning aims?

By the end of the unit, students will be able to:

- explain the main features of the mystery genre and draw on them in their own writing
- use a range of reading strategies, including inference and deduction, to explore layers of meaning
- recognize and comment on the effects of writers' language choices, literary techniques, and grammatical features
- explore and experiment with story structure
- experiment with different narrative viewpoints to create convincing characters, settings, and plots, using a range of literary techniques.

How will this be assessed?

Key assessment task	Focus for assessment
Student Book: Writing a short story in the mystery genre for publication online.	<ul><li>Using the conventions of the mystery genre imaginatively.</li><li>Creating a convincing narrative voice.</li><li>Using a range of vocabulary, sentence structures and punctuation precisely.</li></ul>
Kerboodle: Reading analysis of an extract from 'The Woman in the Big Hat' by Baroness Orczy.	<ul><li>Commenting on plot and text structure, evaluating how effectively these are presented.</li><li>Recognizing how setting is created and how suspense is built.</li><li>Commenting on characterization, supporting ideas with relevant details from the text.</li></ul>

The end-of-unit assessment on Kerboodle can be used either instead of or in addition to the Student Book end-of-unit assessment.

Note that short Progress Checks also feature in this unit, providing formative assessment opportunities to support students' learning.

Lesson sequence   This is a suggested lesson sequence, but you might choose to alter or add to it to suit your particular teaching needs.

Introducing the unit

1 Why Read Mysteries?

- Share existing knowledge of the mystery genre.
- Respond to the Ignite interview featuring Christopher Edge.
- Consider why readers may be attracted to particular genres.
- Write a short article encouraging readers to read books from students' own favourite genres.

---

2 What Makes a Mystery?	**3 Reading Detective**	**4 A Sense of Mystery**
• Identify the typical features of the mystery genre. • Read an extract from 'The Adventure of the Speckled Band', looking at genre features and characterization. • Role-play the scene, drawing on predictions about the story.	• Use inference and deduction to explore layers of meaning. • Re-read the extract from 'The Adventure of the Speckled Band'. • Write an analysis of inferences made, supported by quotations.	• Explore how vocabulary and subordinate clauses can be used to create suspense. • Read an extract from 'The Adventure of the Speckled Band'. • Write the next paragraphs of the story, using techniques explored to create suspense.

5 Real-life Mysteries	**6 Plotting the Perfect Crime**	**7 Watching the Detectives**
• Investigate how you can take inspiration from real-life events to create your own mystery story. • Read a newspaper report about a jewellery theft. • Role-play and write the opening scene of a story based on the report.	• Explore how to structure a mystery story. • Read a non-fiction text about detection techniques. • Devise and shape the plot for a mystery story based around a theft.	• Explore characterization in extracts from different mystery stories. • Read extracts from *The Big Sleep*, *A Study in Scarlet*, and *The Ruby in the Smoke* to explore how character is created. • Write a description of a fictional detective.

8 Scene of the Crime	**9 Step into the Mystery**	**10 Assessment**
• Explore how writers create effective narrative voices. • Read an extract from *The Secret History*. • Rewrite the extract as a third-person narrative.	• Use role play and creative writing to explore setting and situation. • Read an extract from *The London Eye Mystery*. • Use photographs to write a character into a setting.	• Student Book: Plan, draft, edit and proofread a short mystery story. • Kerboodle: Read and analyse an extract from 'The Woman in the Big Hat' by Baroness Orczy.

Preparing to teach

Refresh your knowledge

You might find it helpful to refer to the following key points when planning your teaching of this unit.

- The mystery is synonymous with stories of crime, but the genre can also include thrillers, stories of the supernatural and detective fiction.
- The roots of the mystery genre can be traced back to the 18th century: stories of real-life crime in the *Newgate Calendar* and the influence of gothic novels, such as *The Mysteries of Udolpho* by Ann Radcliffe.
- In the first half of the 19th century, the public appetite for stories about crime and mystery led to the publication of 'penny dreadfuls' – inexpensive novels issued in instalments and filled with lurid tales of murder and the macabre.
- *The Murders in the Rue Morgue*, a short story written by Edgar Allan Poe in 1841, is considered by many to be the first classic mystery. It introduced features that now define the genre: a puzzling crime, a masterful detective and an ingenious solution.
- Mystery fiction grew in popularity in the latter half of the 19th century, as adult literacy rose as a result of the *Education Act* (1870), and popular monthly magazines were established. These magazines contained a blend of stories, articles and pictures. The stories had to be read in short episodes, but still keep the reader interested, which popularized the mystery in the short-story form.
- In *The Strand Magazine*, Sir Arthur Conan Doyle created a new style of hero for the mystery genre – in the form of Sherlock Holmes (a detective who solved mysteries by applying his deductive skills).
- In the 20th century, the mystery genre continued to evolve into new sub-genres, including: the cosy or manor-house mystery, popularized in the novels of Agatha Christie; hard-boiled detective fiction from American writers, such as Raymond Chandler; and mysteries set in different cultures, such as Alexander McCall Smith's *The No.1 Ladies' Detective Agency*. Mysteries are also popular in children's fiction, for example the Sally Lockhart sequence of novels by Philip Pullman.

Links and further reading

- The website of the literary estate of Sir Arthur Conan Doyle contains a biography, bibliography and information about his most famous creation: www.sherlockholmesonline.org/index.htm
- The following website contains information about Victorian publishing, including 'penny dreadfuls' and monthly magazines: http://www.bl.uk/collections/early/victorian/intro.html
- This website gives an overview of the mystery and crime fiction genre: http://www.thereadingclub.co.uk/crimeandmystery.html
- Further reading: *Vintage Mystery and Detective Stories*, edited by David Stuart Davies.

- Recommendations for students' independent reading: *The Ruby in the Smoke* by Philip Pullman; *Montmorency* by Eleanor Updale; *The Diamond of Drury Lane* by Julia Golding; *Twelve Minutes to Midnight* by Christopher Edge; *A Gathering Light* by Jennifer Donnelly; *The Hound of the Baskervilles* by Arthur Conan Doyle; *The Curious Incident of the Dog in the Night-Time* by Mark Haddon; *The Moonstone* by Wilkie Collins; *Moonfleet* by J. Meade Falkner.

Please note that OUP is not responsible for third-party content. Although all links were correct at the time of publication, the content and location of this material may change.

Planning guidance and teaching tips

Think about how you can make the materials relevant to your students and responsive to their needs. Some suggested approaches to address key areas are provided below.

- Although mystery fiction can be a motivating genre, reading a Victorian short story can create challenges for **more-reluctant readers**, as well as **EAL** students. Be prepared to work with these students in one-to-one and guided group contexts to support their reading of extracts from 'The Adventure of the Speckled Band'.

- Students will use a range of reading strategies to engage with and respond to the texts in this unit, but a key focus is to develop their skills of **inference** and **deduction** to help them explore layers of meaning. Ensure that they know the distinction between 'inference' and 'deduction'. Deduction is a judgement about something based on given information; inferences are opinions and hypotheses that draw on prior knowledge, personal engagement and clues. Generally, inference requires more-complex reasoning by the reader.

- Provide students with appropriate **differentiated** support for their writing, using the Kerboodle resources. Skills-based resources have been provided which link to this unit. Select resources that will develop areas of weakness in students' writing. Ensure an appropriate level of challenge for **gifted and talented** students, e.g. by encouraging more-confident writers to experiment with the conventions of the genre in their writing, such as revealing the identity of the murderer at the outset of the story.

- Allow time in the classroom for students to talk about and reflect on their independent reading. Creating opportunities for students to discuss and share ideas about a text can help to engage **more-reluctant readers** and dispel their negative attitudes about reading.

- Encourage students, in small groups, to draw on their independent reading to produce a reading trail for the mystery genre. This could be displayed in the school library to promote **reading for pleasure**.

- Refer to the **Grammar Reference Guide** on Kerboodle for definitions and exemplars of the specific grammar and punctuation terms covered in this unit (as highlighted by the Literacy icon). Kerboodle also provides **SPAG interactives** to help improve the technical accuracy of students' writing and the application of grammar in context.

- The final assessment task can help to motivate students' writing, and also provide opportunities for students to work with real writers. You could make further use of the **Ignite Interview** with Christopher Edge in the Student Book (or play the Ignite Interview films on Kerboodle). The Christopher Edge interview provides insights into the writing process. However, you could also provide further inspiration and support by arranging for an author of mystery stories to come into the classroom to share their perspective and advice as a writer.

Lesson focus

Why are we teaching this?

Lesson 1 launches the 'It's a Mystery' unit by introducing the study of the genre. Students consider and use their prior knowledge of the mystery genre to create a list of typical features; evaluate arguments put forward for reading this genre; and reflect on their own independent reading.

What are students learning?

Students will be able to:

- consider why readers may be attracted to particular genres.

How you could teach this

A variety of activities and approaches are provided on the right for you to select from and adapt to meet the needs of your students. The Kerboodle lesson player sequence is derived from these suggestions, to act as a starting point for your lesson.

Answers

Answers to Student Book activities, where relevant, can be found on page 39.

Teaching suggestions

Ignition

Ignite English interview

You might like to play Ignite Interview Film 1 to the class. In this film we are introduced to Christopher Edge, mystery writer, and his thoughts about mystery writing. Before playing the film, ask students to identify and list the reasons Christopher gives in the film for reading and writing mystery stories. After playing the film, ask students to reflect on their own reading and why they choose particular types of books.

Resources

Kerboodle: 1 Ignite Interview Christopher Edge Film 1

Mystery reading

Ask students, in pairs or small groups, to discuss any mystery stories they may have watched or read. Encourage them to articulate what they enjoyed most about these stories, and also to identify those features of the mystery genre with the most appeal.

Resources

Student Book 2: Activities 1 and 2, page 9

Genre check

Check that all students can define the term 'genre'. Ask students to identify synonyms for the mystery genre, e.g. crime fiction, detective fiction, etc.

Exploration

The history of the mystery

Use 'The history of the mystery' presentation on Kerboodle to discuss the literary and historical context of the mystery genre.

Resources

Kerboodle: 1.1 The history of the mystery

Why read mysteries?

Discuss the mystery genre's popularity, either as a whole class, in pairs or in groups. Support differentiation by giving lower-achieving students statements to argue for or against, e.g. 'Everybody loves a good murder'; 'It's fun to work out the mystery yourself'. Alternatively, you could use the 'Why read mysteries' presentation on Kerboodle to prompt the discussion.

Resources

Student Book 2: Activity 1, page 10

Kerboodle: 1.1 Why read mysteries?

Essay analysis

Use shared reading to identify and annotate the stylistic features of the essay by K. K. Beck – exploring how information about the genre is interleaved with Beck's arguments outlining the appeal of detective fiction, and recommendations for reading within it. Discuss how students should draw on these techniques in their own writing.

and guidance

Consolidation

Mystery in the library

Discuss what makes an effective slogan. Visit the school library to look at the existing displays and slogans used to encourage students to read. Look at the mystery books that are available for students to borrow.

Resources
Student Book 2: Activity 2, page 10

Genre word clouds

Use an online word cloud tool, such as the weblink below, to generate word clouds for different genres. You could paste the texts from books of different genres into the word cloud generator to identify whether any of the key words that students have used to describe the genre are generated.

Resources
Student Book 2: Activity 3a, page 10

Weblink: www.wordle.net

Cover clues

Show the class the 'Book covers' image gallery on Kerboodle and ask students to identify the genre of each book from its cover, as well as highlighting the clues (title, cover image, author, font style, etc.) on which they based their decisions.

Resources
Kerboodle: 1.1 Book covers

Recommended reads

Ask the School Librarian to recommend suitable mystery books that students could read.

Social reading

Ask students to create 140-character tweets to recommend their favourite reads (not necessarily from the mystery genre). You could share these using the school's VLE.

News reporter skills

As a class, discuss and agree the top three reasons for reading mystery stories.

Extra Time

Ask students to read and review a mystery story of their choice.

Lesson focus

Why are we teaching this?

This lesson enables students to explore the typical features of the mystery genre. Sherlock Holmes is arguably the most iconic detective ever created, and, by reading an extract from the classic short story 'The Adventure of the Speckled Band', students investigate how the features of the genre are introduced and begin to explore characterization.

What are students learning?

Students will be able to:
- identify the typical features of the mystery genre.

How you could teach this

A variety of activities and approaches are provided on the right for you to select from and adapt to meet the needs of your students. The Kerboodle lesson player sequence is derived from these suggestions, to act as a starting point for your lesson.

Teaching suggestions

Ignition

Features of a mystery

Show the 'What makes a mystery?' presentation on Kerboodle. Ask students to identify examples of typical mystery genre features in any mystery stories they have already read or watched.

Resources

Kerboodle: 1.2 What makes a mystery?

Activate prior knowledge

Ask students to share any prior knowledge they may have about Sherlock Holmes. Create a list of adjectives to describe the detective.

Sherlock Holmes

Show a trailer for the BBC TV series *Sherlock*. Ask students to share their views about the character – drawing on details from the trailer to support their assertions.

Resources

Weblink: http://www.bbc.co.uk/programmes/p008wpcb

Exploration

The mystery begins

Use shared reading to identify and annotate the typical features of the mystery genre when reading the extract from 'The Adventure of the Speckled Band' in the Student Book.

Resources

Student Book 2: Activity 1, page 12

Impressions of characters

Ask students to use the 'Character impressions' worksheet on Kerboodle to explore their initial impressions about the characters of both Holmes and the mysterious woman. Encourage them to select details from the extract in the Student Book to support the impressions they share.

Resources

Student Book 2: Activity 2, page 12

Kerboodle: 1.2 Character impressions

Vocabulary builder

Encourage students to use a range of strategies to work out the meaning of any new or unfamiliar vocabulary from the extract of 'The Adventure of the Speckled Band' in the Student Book, e.g. reading on and looking back to find contextual clues, etc.

Answers

Answers to Student Book activities, where relevant, can be found on page 39.

and guidance

Consolidation

Cracking the case

As a class, discuss students' predictions about what this case will be about. Then hold a class vote with the aim of identifying the most popular prediction.

Resources
Student Book 2: Activity 3, page 12

Role-play

Ask students, working in pairs, to role-play the meeting between Sherlock Holmes and the mysterious woman. Encourage them to use tone, intonation and action to show the characters' feelings – drawing on details from the extract in the Student Book to continue the conversation.

Resources
Student Book 2: Activity 4, page 12

Adapting the scene

Ask students to turn the extract in the Student Book into a play script. Revise the conventions for the presentation of stage directions, dialogue, etc. in play scripts. Encourage higher-achieving students to continue their play scripts by drawing on their role-plays from Activity 4 in the Student Book.

Performance

Select several pairs of students to perform the role-plays they prepared in response to Activity 4 in the Student Book. Then, as a class, discuss the different ways in which the pairs continued the conversation between Holmes and the mysterious woman. Which conversation seemed the most plausible, given the evidence so far?

Personal response

Ask students to discuss their own feelings about the story so far and evaluate the impact that it has had on them as readers.

Commandments

Show the class 'The ten commandments of detective fiction' presentation on Kerboodle (explaining that it was written by Ronald Knox in 1928; hence its slightly politically incorrect nature to modern readers). Then ask students to create their own five commandments for the mystery genre.

Resources
Kerboodle: 1.2 The ten commandments of detective fiction

Extra Time

Ask students to read the whole of 'The Adventure of the Speckled Band'. The full version of this text is available on Kerboodle.

Lesson focus

Why are we teaching this?

Students need to be able to read texts which are increasingly challenging – using their skills of inference and deduction to explore layers of meaning, as well as understanding how to refer to evidence from the text. As a pre-1914 text, the extract from 'The Adventure of the Speckled Band' on page 13 of the Student Book is sufficiently demanding for students to apply their skills of inference and deduction, not least because it demonstrates Sherlock Holmes using his own deductive skills.

What are students learning?

Students will be able to:

- use inference and deduction to explore layers of meaning.

How you could teach this

A variety of activities and approaches are provided on the right for you to select from and adapt to meet the needs of your students. The Kerboodle lesson player sequence is derived from these suggestions to act as a starting point for your lesson.

Answers

Answers to Student Book activities, where relevant, can be found on page 39.

Teaching suggestions

Ignition

Inference and deduction

Ask students to define the terms 'inference' and 'deduction'. Draw out distinctions between the two:

- Deduction is a judgement about something, based on information from the text.

- Inferences are opinions and hypotheses drawing on prior knowledge, personal engagement and clues from the text.

Use the 'Inference' interactive activity on Kerboodle to test students' understanding of this term.

Resources
Kerboodle: 1.3 Inference

Mystery mash-up

Give students 'The case of the disappearing grandmother' worksheet on Kerboodle, which has been written as a Sherlock Holmes mystery. Ask them to deduce the case that Sherlock Holmes is investigating here, and also to identify the clues that Holmes finds and uses to make his deductions.

Resources
Kerboodle: 1.3 The case of the disappearing grandmother

Murder mystery

Use masking tape to create the outline of a body on the classroom floor and leave 'clues' next to it, such as a spanner, a length of rope, a cryptic note. Ask students to deduce what has happened.

Exploration

Close reading

Model close reading of the extract from 'The Adventure of the Speckled Band' on page 13 of the Student Book, with the aim of identifying clues about the mysterious woman. Encourage students to discuss any inferences that can be made from these clues by exploring different layers of meaning.

Resources
Student Book 2: Activity 1, page 14

Forensic analysis

Challenge higher-achieving students to use the 'Forensic analysis' worksheet on Kerboodle to develop a more-detailed analysis of the mysterious woman's character.

Resources
Student Book 2: Activities 2 and 3, page 15

Kerboodle: 1.3 Forensic analysis

Writing your analysis

Model how to write a paragraph explaining the inferences made about the character of the woman in black. Highlight how to draw different details together to build a more-detailed analysis (integrating quotation with comment).

Resources
Student Book 2: Activity 4, page 15

and guidance

 ## Consolidation

Debating the detective

Hold a classroom debate on the question: 'Is Sherlock Holmes the greatest fictional detective?'. Give students time to prepare their contributions for the debate. Encourage them to consider the character's cultural impact as well as his characteristics as a detective.

Advertising Sherlock Holmes

Display some examples of Victorian advertisements. Ask students to create a print advertisement for Sherlock Holmes's detective agency.

Resources

Weblink: http://www.bl.uk/learning/histcitizen/victorians/popculture/culture.html

Evaluating openings

Discuss the standard story-opening formula for Sherlock Holmes cases – a potential client visits Sherlock Holmes at Baker Street to present him with a possible new case. Ask students to rate the extract on page 13 of the Student Book as the opening of a detective novel. Then ask them to draw on examples from their own reading to discuss other ways in which the story could have been started.

Ignite English interview

You might like to play Ignite Interview Film 1 to the class. In this film we are introduced to Christopher Edge and his thoughts about mystery writing.

Resources

Kerboodle: 1 Ignite Interview Christopher Edge Film 1

Progress check

Ask students, working in pairs, to swap the paragraphs they wrote in response to Activity 4 in the Student Book. Encourage them to praise two strong aspects and to suggest one area for improvement in their partner's analysis.

Licensed to infer

Ask students to create a checklist of the skills that a reading detective needs. Share as a class and agree a list of the top three skills.

Extra Time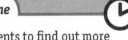

Ask students to find out more about Sherlock Holmes and his creator, Sir Arthur Conan Doyle. Also ask them to think about why Sherlock Holmes stories have been (and continue to be) so popular.

Lesson focus

Why are we teaching this?

A key feature of mystery fiction is the creation of suspense. The extract from 'The Adventure of the Speckled Band' on page 16 of the Student Book allows students to explore the literary and grammatical techniques that are used to create a tense and unsettling atmosphere – and to learn how to apply these techniques to their own writing.

What are students learning?

Students will be able to:

- explore how vocabulary and subordinate clauses can be used to create suspense.

How you could teach this

A variety of activities and approaches are provided on the right for you to select from and adapt to meet the needs of your students. The Kerboodle lesson player sequence is derived from these suggestions, to act as a starting point for your lesson.

Teaching suggestions

Ignition

What is suspense?

Ask students to explain what 'suspense' is. Encourage them to provide concrete examples of suspense being created effectively in books or films they may have read or seen.

Suspenseful scene

Show students the 'kitchen scene' from the film *Jurassic Park*. Ask them to rate the scene from 1 to 10, according to the level of suspense they think it creates. Discuss the elements that create this atmosphere of tension.

Resources

Search online for the video clip of the kitchen scene from *Jurassic Park*.

A tense situation

Give students a situation, such as a person being woken up at night by a strange sound downstairs. Discuss how they would film that scene to create a sense of suspense.

Exploration

Tension graph

Ask students to use the 'Extract tension graph' worksheet on Kerboodle to create a tension graph showing the increasing tension throughout the extract from 'The Adventure of the Speckled Band' on page 16 of the Student Book.

Resources

Kerboodle: 1.4 Extract tension graph

Phrases and clauses

Use the 'Phrases and clauses' worksheet on Kerboodle to extend students' learning.

Resources

Student Book 2: Activity 1, page 17

Kerboodle: 1.4 Phrases and clauses

Storyboarding the scene

Ask students to use the 'Storyboarding the scene' worksheet on Kerboodle to storyboard the scene described in the extract on page 16 of the Student Book for a film adaptation of 'The Adventure of the Speckled Band'. Ask them to consider how camera shots, lighting, sound and music could be used to create a suspenseful scene.

Resources

Kerboodle: 1.4 Storyboarding the scene

Answers

Answers to Student Book activities, where relevant, can be found on page 39.

 Lesson Player   Image  Video   Worksheet

and guidance

Consolidation

Shared reading

Use shared reading to identify and annotate the vocabulary and grammatical features that have been used to create a tense and unsettling atmosphere in the extract on page 16 of the Student Book.

Resources
Student Book 2: Activity 2, page 17

Modelled writing

Model writing the next paragraph of the story. Articulate which grammatical and vocabulary choices you are making in order to create a sense of suspense.

Resources
Student Book 2: Activity 3, page 17

Vocabulary builder

Ask students to identify any challenging vocabulary in the extract on page 16 of the Student Book. Tell them to use a dictionary when necessary to look up any awkward definitions. Then ask them to create their own suspenseful sentences, using the vocabulary identified.

Audio reading

Ask students to create an audio reading of the extract on page 16 of the Student Book for a 'Book at bedtime' feature on a radio programme. Encourage them to consider how they could use tone and intonation to help build a sense of suspense during the reading.

Progress Check

Ask students, working in pairs, to swap and assess the paragraphs they wrote in response to Activity 3 in the Student Book, using the 'Progress Check assessment' worksheet on Kerboodle. Ask them to highlight any examples of vocabulary and sentence structure which they could use to justify their ratings.

Resources
Kerboodle: 1.4 Progress check assessment

Predictions

Ask students to provide theories about how Julia Stoner died. Encourage them to draw on evidence from the text to support their theories.

What happened next?

Ask students to read the next section of 'The Adventure of the Speckled Band'. Then discuss how successfully the atmosphere of suspense has been sustained.

Resources
Kerboodle: 1.4 'The Adventure of the Speckled Band'

Extra Time

Ask students, if they haven't already done so, to finish reading *The Adventure of the Speckled Band*. The full version of this text is available on Kerboodle.

Weblink   Presentation   Interactive activity

Lesson focus

Why are we teaching this?

Creative writing is often a process shrouded in mystery. This lesson provides students with the opportunity to explore a source of authorial inspiration – drawing on real-life events and stories to inspire their own creative writing.

What are students learning?

Students will be able to:

- investigate how to take inspiration from real-life events to create their own mystery story.

How you could teach this

A variety of activities and approaches are provided on the right for you to select from and adapt to meet the needs of your students. The Kerboodle lesson player sequence is derived from these suggestions, to act as a starting point for your lesson.

Answers

Answers to Student Book activities, where relevant, can be found on page 39.

Teaching suggestions

Ignition

Newspaper headlines

Provide students with a selection of recent newspaper headlines and reports. Ask them to discuss how those reports could inspire stories. Make connections and join ideas as students share their suggestions.

Resources

A selection of recent newspaper headlines and reports

It's a heist

Ask students to explain what a 'heist' is. Agree a class definition and ask them to suggest fictional crimes that would fit this definition, e.g. a bank robbery, etc.

Exploration

Crime/fiction

Discuss how real-life crimes sometimes inspire authors. For example, 'The Tell-Tale Heart' by Edgar Allen Poe and *Murder on the Orient Express* by Agatha Christie, which have both been referenced on the weblink below.

Resources

Student Book 2: Activity 1, page 18

Weblink: http://www.stylist. co.uk/books/8-real-crimes-that-inspired-fiction

Model reading

Model reading the newspaper report on page 19 of the Student Book about the Cannes jewellery heist. Identify details from the report that students could use in their own stories, by referring to the typical features of a mystery, e.g. a crime – the jewellery heist, a detective – the police commander, suspects – the Chopard employee, etc.

🏠 Lesson Player   📷 Image   🎞 Video   📄 Worksheet

and guidance

Consolidation

Planning a story

Ask students to discuss ways in which selected details from the newspaper report on page 19 of the Student Book could be changed or adapted to give their own stories an original twist. Use the 'Planning a story' worksheet on Kerboodle to support students who need extra help with this.

Resources

Student Book 2: Activity 2, page 18

Kerboodle: 1.5 Planning a story

Role-play

Ensure that students prepare for their role-play activity by discussing the interview questions they could ask each person in role. You might want to agree a class list of key questions that need to be answered.

Resources

Student Book 2: Activity 3, page 18

Effective openings

Discuss what makes an effective opening to a story. The 'Effective openings' presentation on Kerboodle will help students to identify techniques and approaches to use in their own writing when they complete Activity 4 in the Student Book.

Resources

Student Book 2: Activity 4, page 18

Kerboodle: 1.5 Effective openings

Progress check

Ask students, working in pairs, to assess each other's story openings in response to Activity 4 in the Student Book – using the 'Effective openings' presentation on Kerboodle as a checklist.

Resources

Kerboodle: 1.5 Effective openings

Performance

Choose several pairs of students to perform the role-plays they prepared in response to Activity 3 in the Student Book. As a class, identify any interesting details that each pair shared, and discuss ways in which they could be incorporated into a story.

Inspirations

Create a class list of possible sources of inspiration for students' writing, e.g. news stories, places they have visited, overheard conversations, etc.

Extra Time

Ask students to continue writing their mystery stories.

Lesson focus

Why are we teaching this?

The formula that underpins many mystery stories makes it an ideal genre to explore story structure. This lesson allows students to move from analysing the plot of a classic mystery story, *The Mysterious Affair at Styles* by Agatha Christie, to building the plot for their own mystery story – drawing on details from a non-fiction text about crime scene investigation to inspire and add verisimilitude to their writing.

What are students learning?

Students will be able to:

- explore how to structure a mystery story.

How you could teach this

A variety of activities and approaches are provided on the right for you to select from and adapt to meet the needs of your students. The Kerboodle lesson player sequence is derived from these suggestions, to act as a starting point for your lesson.

Answers

Answers to Student Book activities, where relevant, can be found on page 39.

Teaching suggestions

Ignition

Revising features of a mystery

Use the Lesson 2 'What makes a mystery?' presentation on Kerboodle to revise the typical features of the mystery genre. Discuss the structure of mystery stories, e.g. discovery of crime, following clues, resolution of mystery.

Resources
Kerboodle: 1.2 What makes a mystery?

Red herring

Ask students to explain what a 'red herring' is. Discuss the etymology of the phrase, e.g. a smoked herring supposedly used by fugitives to throw bloodhounds off the scent of their trail. Explore alternative phrases with similar meanings, e.g. smoke screen, curve ball, wild-goose chase, etc.

Plot twist

Ask students to define the term 'plot twist' and suggest examples from any mystery stories they might have watched or seen.

Exploration

Reading club podcast

Play the Fun Kids Book Club podcast to the class from the weblink below, and then ask students to create a podcast of their own about a mystery story they have read. This could be about an extract they read earlier in the unit, or a story from their independent reading.

Resources
Weblink: http://www.funkidslive.com/podcasts/the-fun-kids-book-club-twelve-minutes-to-midnight/

The shape of a mystery

Use 'The shape of a mystery' presentation on Kerboodle to analyse the structure of typical mystery stories. Discuss sub-genres, such as 'locked room' mysteries, police procedurals, etc. and ask students which they prefer and why.

Resources
Kerboodle: 1.6 The shape of a mystery

Plotting the mystery

Encourage higher-achieving students to use the 'Plotting the mystery' worksheet on Kerboodle to analyse the plots of any other mystery stories which they may have read or seen.

Resources
Kerboodle: 1.6 Plotting the mystery

and guidance

Consolidation

Visual plots

Model plotting the selected details from Activity 1 in the Student Book onto the graph. Ask students to identify the clues and plot twists. Discuss your decisions when sequencing the details on the graph.

Resources
Student Book 2: Activity 1, page 21

Climax

Ask the class to discuss what the climax of the story will reveal, and then vote on alternative endings. Share the actual ending of the Agatha Christie story, using the weblink below, and discuss whether students think this is an effective climax.

Resources
Student Book 2: Activity 2, page 21

Weblink: http://en.wikipedia.org/wiki/The_Mysterious_Affair_at_Styles

Trace evidence

Ask students to read the 'Tell-tale marks' paragraph of the extract on page 21 of the Student Book. Discuss ways in which the clues could be incorporated into the story. Ask them to suggest other possible sources of trace evidence – activating cross-curricular knowledge from Science.

Resources
Student Book 2: Activity 3, page 21

Plotting the story

Emphasize that the story students are plotting for Activity 3 could be the story they write for the final unit assessment in Lesson 10. Also refer them back to the related work they have already completed in Lesson 5.

Clues and red herrings

Ask student volunteers to share some of the clues from the plots of their stories. The class could vote on whether they think they are real clues or red herrings.

A dramatic opening

Ask some students to share their ideas for dramatic openings to their stories. Discuss the effectiveness of these openings.

Extra Time

Ask students to analyse the structure of another mystery story. This could be a short story, TV programme or film.

Lesson focus

Why are we teaching this?

The creation of convincing characters is a key component of a successful mystery story. This lesson allows students to study characterization in three contrasting texts: *A Study in Scarlet* by Arthur Conan Doyle, *The Big Sleep* by Raymond Chandler, and *The Ruby in the Smoke* by Philip Pullman. As well as developing their critical-reading skills, students can apply the narrative and grammatical techniques explored in these extracts to create their own fictional detectives.

What are students learning?

Students will be able to:

- explore characterization in extracts from different mystery stories.

How you could teach this

A variety of activities and approaches are provided on the right for you to select from and adapt to meet the needs of your students. The Kerboodle lesson player sequence is derived from these suggestions, to act as a starting point for your lesson.

Answers

Answers to Student Book activities, where relevant, can be found on page 39.

Teaching suggestions

Ignition

Fictional detectives

Ask students to name any fictional detectives they know from the page and screen, e.g. Miss Marple, Sherlock Holmes, etc. Compare and contrast the different character traits that these characters possess.

What makes a good detective?

Discuss what makes a good detective. Encourage students to link the adjectives they choose with any fictional detectives they are aware of.

Using the 'Equipment for a detective' interactive activity on Kerboodle, ask students to discuss and rank the items in terms of importance. Encourage students to justify their suggestions.

Resources

Student Book 2: Activity 1, page 22

Kerboodle: 1.7 Equipment for a detective

Teacher in role

Working in role, interview students for the job of a private investigator. Ask questions that encourage them to consider the skills required in this role.

Exploration

First- and third-person narrative

Use the 'First- and third-person narrative' presentation on Kerboodle to explore the different techniques that can be used to portray character from these two narrative perspectives.

Resources

Kerboodle: 1.7 First- and third-person narrative

Detectives gallery

Ask students to read the short extracts from *A Study in Scarlet* and *The Big Sleep* on page 23 of the Student Book. Then display the 'Detectives on screen' image gallery from Kerboodle and ask students to select the image of each detective that best reflects the perception which they have built up of him from the extract. Encourage them to refer to textual details to support their selections.

Resources

Student Book 2: Activity 2, page 23

Kerboodle: 1.7 Detectives on screen

Ignite English interview

You might like to play Ignite Interview Film 2 to the class, in which Christopher Edge discusses writing tips.

Resources

Kerboodle: 1 Ignite Interview Christopher Edge Film 2

 Lesson Player   Image   Video   Worksheet

and guidance

| Consolidation |

Philip Marlowe in focus

Ask students to read the two additional extracts from *The Big Sleep* provided on Kerboodle. Discuss how these extracts develop students' understanding of Philip Marlowe's character, and also the techniques that the author, Raymond Chandler, uses to do this.

Resources

Kerboodle: 1.7 *The Big Sleep* additional extracts

Personal response

Encourage students to explore their personal responses to both extracts on page 23 of the Student Book – reflecting on which story they would be more likely to choose as a reader. Display covers and blurbs for *The Big Sleep* and *A Study in Scarlet*, and discuss what impact they might have on students' reading choices.

Resources

Student Book 2: Activity 3, page 23

Search online book retailers for front covers and blurbs

Character profile

Use the 'Character profile' worksheet on Kerboodle to support lower-achieving students when creating their fictional detective.

Resources

Student Book 2: Activity 4, page 23

Kerboodle: 1.7 Character profile

Model reading

Model reading the extract from *The Ruby in the Smoke* on page 25 of the Student Book. Identify details that help the reader to learn about Sally's character, e.g. her appearance – 'uncommonly pretty', her family – 'dressed in mourning'/'sorry to hear about your father', etc.

Resources

Student Book: Activity 6a, page 24

Punctuation

Use the 'Pullman's punctuation' worksheet on Kerboodle to explore the use of punctuation in the extract from *The Ruby in the Smoke* on page 25 of the Student Book.

Resources

Student Book: Activity 6b, page 24

Kerboodle: 1.7 Pullman's punctuation

Model writing

Model writing the next few lines of the story, as required in the Extra Time activity on page 25 of the Student Book. Articulate the writing choices you are making to help create a picture of Sally in the reader's mind – including descriptive details, and conveying a sense of character through dialogue and other characters' reactions.

Resources

Student Book 2: Extra Time, page 25

Consolidation

The detective factor

Ask students to share descriptions of the fictional detectives they created for Activities 4a and 4b in the Student Book. Ask the class to vote for the best detective – according to the character traits previously identified as important.

A detective needs to be …

Ask students to create a checklist of character traits for a successful detective.

Progress Check

Ask students, working in pairs, to swap their continuations of the extract from *The Ruby in the Smoke* (completed as part of the Extra Time activity). Encourage them to identify two ways in which character has been revealed, and also to suggest one area for improvement in their partner's writing.

Extra Time

Ask students how the story of *The Ruby in the Smoke* might continue, before asking them to write the next ten lines of the story.

 Weblink   Presentation    Interactive activity

Lesson focus

Why are we teaching this?

The mystery genre encompasses a wide range of settings, from the historical to the contemporary. This lesson allows students to study how setting is created in the novel *The Secret History* by Donna Tartt, and also to explore how this can be interleaved with the depiction of character via narrative voice and the delivery of plot details.

What are students learning?

Students will be able to:

- explore how writers create effective narrative voices.

How you could teach this

A variety of activities and approaches are provided on the right for you to select from and adapt to meet the needs of your students. The Kerboodle lesson player sequence is derived from these suggestions, to act as a starting point for your lesson.

Teaching suggestions

Ignition

Describing place

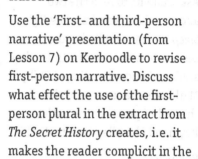

Ask students to look around the classroom and make notes about the setting. Encourage them to draw on each of their senses as they note down the details and use them to write a brief description of the setting.

Reading journal/Writing notebook

Discuss how students can use a journal to reflect on their reading, e.g. noting down powerful descriptions, favourite lines, questions and thoughts. Link to how authors use journals to gather inspiration, e.g. descriptions of characters/places, collecting photographs, etc.

Fictional settings

Read an extract from one of your favourite novels and discuss the setting described. Ask students to share the settings of their favourite stories, e.g. Middle Earth in *The Lord of the Rings*, Victorian London in *The Ruby in the Smoke*.

Exploration

Revising first-person narrative

Use the 'First- and third-person narrative' presentation (from Lesson 7) on Kerboodle to revise first-person narrative. Discuss what effect the use of the first-person plural in the extract from *The Secret History* creates, i.e. it makes the reader complicit in the crime, etc.

Resources

Student Book 2: Activity 1, page 27

Kerboodle: 1.7 First- and third-person narrative

Model reading

Re-read the extract from *The Secret History* on page 26 of the Student Book – identifying details included by the writer to build the setting. Highlight how setting, plot and characterization are interleaved in the extract and discuss the effects of this.

Resources

Student Book 2: Activity 2, page 27

Answers

Answers to Student Book activities, where relevant, can be found on page 39.

and guidance

Consolidation

Sentence structure

Ask students to use the 'Sentence structure' worksheet on Kerboodle to analyse the use of colons, semi-colons and commas in the final sentence of the extract on page 26 of the Student Book.

Resources

Student Book 2: Activity 3b, page 27

Kerboodle: 1.8 Sentence structure

Model writing

Model rewriting the opening of the extract as a third-person narrative. Highlight the changes you are making and discuss the impact of these on the reader, e.g. 'It was only when the snow in the mountains started to melt that the body was discovered ...'.

Resources

Student Book 2: Activity 4, page 27

Story openings

Ask students to write the opening of a story where the narrator confesses to something, e.g. stealing a younger sibling's clothes, etc. Encourage students to draw on the techniques explored in the extract from *The Secret History* on page 26 of the Student Book.

Personal response

Ask students to read the extended opening extract from *The Secret History* on Kerboodle, and then discuss whether they think this extract is an effective opening for a mystery story. Remind them about the typical features of a mystery story, e.g. a dramatic opening, and discuss whether this extract provides this.

Resources

Kerboodle: 1.8 *The Secret History* extended opening

Progress check

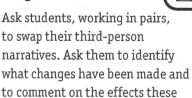

Ask students, working in pairs, to swap their third-person narratives. Ask them to identify what changes have been made and to comment on the effects these changes create.

Top ten settings

Ask the class to suggest and vote on the top ten settings for mystery stories.

Setting tips

Agree a class list of top tips for creating a believable setting.

Extra Time

Ask students to find an extract from a book they are reading that builds an effective setting, and then to write a paragraph analysing how that setting has been created.

Lesson focus

Why are we teaching this?

This lesson allows students to use role-play and creative-writing techniques to explore how they can create believable settings in their own writing. An extract from *The London Eye Mystery* by Siobhan Dowd provides a modern update of the locked-room mystery, and is the stimulus for students' creative engagement in this lesson.

What are students learning?

Students will be able to:

- use role-play and creative writing to explore setting and situation.

How you could teach this

A variety of activities and approaches are provided on the right for you to select from and adapt to meet the needs of your students. The Kerboodle lesson player sequence is derived from these suggestions, to act as a starting point for your lesson.

Answers

Answers to Student Book activities, where relevant, can be found on page 39.

Teaching suggestions

Ignition

Classroom mystery

Tell students that something has been stolen from a locked classroom. Then ask them, working in small groups, to discuss their theories about how and why the object was stolen.

Top tips

Check students' understanding of how setting can be created. Create a checklist of top tips.

Creating setting

Use the 'Creating setting' presentation on Kerboodle to discuss how setting is created in fiction and literary non-fiction texts.

Resources
Kerboodle: 1.9 Creating setting

Exploration

Role-play

Ask students to work in threes to role-play the police interview for Activity 1 in the Student Book. Encourage them to think about the questions they could ask and to draw on details from the text in their responses.

Resources
Student Book 2: Activity 1, page 29

Theories

Discuss as a class how *The London Eye Mystery* can be seen as a modern version of the locked-room mystery. Then ask students to read the additional extract from the text on Kerboodle and discuss, in small groups, the theories it outlines. Ask the groups to suggest their own theories and then hold a class vote on the most likely.

Resources
Student Book 2: Activity 2, page 29

Kerboodle: 1.9 *The London Eye Mystery* additional extract

Ignite English interview

You might like to play Ignite Interview Film 1 to the class. In this film we are introduced to Christopher Edge and his thoughts about mystery writing.

Resources
Kerboodle: 1 Ignite Interview Christopher Edge Film 1

  Lesson Player Image  Video Worksheet

and guidance

Character and setting

Discuss the photographs of characters and settings from Activity 3 in the Student Book. Speculate on who the characters might be, their character traits, and what their reactions to the different settings might be. Use the 'Character and setting' image gallery on Kerboodle to provide additional stimuli for students to write their paragraphs.

Resources
Student Book 2: Activity 3, page 29

Kerboodle: 1.9 Character and setting

Online tools

Show the Ignite interview film on Kerboodle where Christopher Edge discusses using online tools to create descriptions of setting (Ignite interview Film 1). Then ask students to use online maps and tools, such as Google Streetview, to recreate a journey and write a description of it.

Resources
Kerboodle: 1 Ignite Interview Christopher Edge Film 1

Salim's story

Extend the role-play from Activity 1 in the Student Book by interviewing students in role as Salim to find out what has happened to him. Use the additional extract from *The London Eye Mystery* to inform this role-play.

Resources
Kerboodle: 1.9 *The London Eye Mystery* additional extract

Storyboarding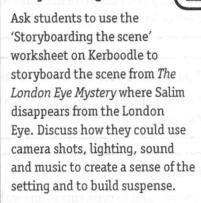

Ask students to use the 'Storyboarding the scene' worksheet on Kerboodle to storyboard the scene from *The London Eye Mystery* where Salim disappears from the London Eye. Discuss how they could use camera shots, lighting, sound and music to create a sense of the setting and to build suspense.

Resources
Kerboodle: 1.9 Storyboarding the scene

Consolidation

Progress Check

Ask students, working in pairs, to assess each other's paragraphs in response to Activity 3 in the Student Book by using the 'Creating setting' presentation on Kerboodle as a checklist to identify the techniques and approaches used.

Resources
Kerboodle: 1.9 Creating setting

Evaluation

Two stars and a wish: ask students to decide on two things they did well and one thing they could improve.

Planning

Ask students to make notes about the setting for their own mystery story (ready for the end-of-unit assessment activity in Lesson 10).

Extra Time

Ask students to read *The London Eye Mystery* or other books by Siobhan Dowd.

Assessment focus

Why are we assessing this?

Students have completed a unit on the mystery genre. While exploring many extracts and examples, they have considered the appeal of the genre and its typical features – studying plot, characterization and setting. They have explored different aspects of writing techniques and completed some initial preparation for their own short mystery story, which they will now plan, draft, edit and proofread in this assessment task.

What are students demonstrating?

Students will be able to:
- plan, draft, edit and proofread a short story.

How to deliver the assessment

Suggestions and guidance on how to set up and prepare your students for the assessment are provided, as well as possible approaches to marking the assessment.

Alternative/additional assessment

There is an alternative end-of-unit assessment available on Kerboodle. This assessment leads to a reading outcome and can be used either in addition to or instead of the Student Book end-of-unit assessment.

Resources
Kerboodle: 1.10 Alternative end-of-unit assessment

Assessment suggestions and guidance

Understanding the assessment

Check that students understand the assessment task. Emphasize that they are being tested on their writing skills and that they can draw on the preparatory work completed earlier in the unit, specifically in Lessons 5, 6, 7 and 9. This task is set as a submission to an e-book anthology of mystery stories. If possible, collate and publish the stories as a class or school anthology using either the school VLE or e-publishing resources.

Resources
Student Book 2: pages 30–31

Planning

Remind students that they will need to choose an appropriate way to plan their work. They should include this plan as part of their assessment.

Completing the assessment

Remind students to edit their first draft and proofread their work. Emphasize that they must complete the assessment individually, so that an accurate mark or level can be given.

Timing and writing expectation

Give students two hours (ideally two lessons) and expect between four to six A4 pages.

Marking

You will want to mark this in line with departmental and school marking guidelines. If you wish, you could use the Ignite English marking scales provided on Kerboodle. Using the Ignite English marking scales will help you to identify specific strengths and areas for improvement in an individual student's writing. This may help you to set development targets as well as building a profile of your class as writers.

Refer to the KS3 National Curriculum and Ignite English mapping grids on pages 154–156 of this Teacher Companion to identify other Ignite English units where these writing skills are covered, or ask students to use the SPAG interactives on Kerboodle to address any areas identified for improvement. The Grammar Reference Guide on Kerboodle contains definitions and additional examples of each of the spelling, punctuation and grammar points covered in the interactives, for your reference.

Resources
Kerboodle: 1 Ignite English marking scales

Kerboodle: SPAG interactives

Kerboodle: Grammar Reference Guide

Key for Kerboodle LRA resources   Worksheet   Interactive activity

Student Book answers

Below are the answers to any largely non-subjective Student Book activities contained within this unit.

Lesson 1

1 Students could identify the following reasons:
- 'pretty much guaranteed that things will happen and the plot will move along'
- characters are forced into action which makes for 'a plot-driven, engaging read'
- readers enjoy the suspense of 'knowing the characters are in danger'
- the reader can detect along with the characters.

Lesson 2

2 Students could comment on the mysterious woman's state of agitation, her nervousness and fear, whilst also identifying Sherlock Holmes's reassuring manner, his perceptiveness and slight air of condescension.

Lesson 3

1 Students could identify the following clues:
- The lady is 'dressed in black and heavily veiled', which implies that she is in mourning.
- She looks old before her time 'her hair was shot with premature grey, and her expression was weary and haggard', which implies that she may have been suffering from great stress and worry recently.
- She is getting married in a month to six weeks, at which point she will gain control of her own finances.

Lesson 4

1 *To Catch a Thief* and *The Bling Ring*.

Lesson 7

2 Students could comment on the tone of Marlowe's narration, striking a matter-of-fact tone mixed with cynical humour, e.g. 'I was neat, clean, shaven and sober, and I didn't care who knew it'.

The description of Holmes in the second extract suggests many of his qualities: his perceptiveness 'eyes sharp and piercing', etc., as well as explicitly identifying several of these, e.g. 'air of alertness and decision', 'man of determination', etc.

6a Students could comment on Sally's youth and beauty, 'sixteen or so – alone, and uncommonly pretty'; the fact that her father is dead; her confidence, 'She tapped on the glass', etc.

Unit 2: Words of War

Unit overview

Why are we teaching this?

In this unit students explore a range of poetry written in response to war. Beginning with a focus on poetry of the First World War, the unit develops by looking at poems prompted by a range of other conflicts, including the Vietnam War, the Cold War, and terrorist attacks.

Through their study of how poets use the genre to express their anger, sorrow, frustration and horror at the consequences of mass conflict, students will widen their understanding of the forms and techniques of poetry.

What are the learning aims?

By the end of the unit, students will be able to:

- understand how a range of poetic techniques are used to create meaning
- explore how poets use language choices to create particular effects
- understand how poetry can reflect the social, cultural and historical context in which it is written
- analyse other text types that also reflect the theme of war
- write a poem in a given form, condensing their ideas through careful word choice
- discuss their ideas with peers to develop and consolidate their learning.

How will this be assessed?

Key assessment task	Focus for assessment
Student Book: Selecting a war poem for illustration by an artist, through consideration of key features such as theme, structure, imagery, mood and tone.	• Analysing meaning in a poem and the effects created for the reader. • Selecting appropriate references to support the analysis.
Kerboodle: Reading the poem 'War Girls' by Jessie Pope and debating the statement: 'War is no place for a woman.'	• Effectively participating in formal debate. • Expressing ideas with clarity and keeping to the point. • Summarizing contributions from others and building on what has been said.

The end-of-unit assessment on Kerboodle can be used either instead of or in addition to the Student Book end-of-unit assessment.

Note that short Progress Checks also feature in this unit, providing formative assessment opportunities to support students' learning.

Lesson sequence

This is a suggested lesson sequence, but you might choose to alter or add to it to suit your particular teaching needs.

Introducing the unit

1 Joining Up

- Adapt and use existing knowledge of the vocabulary of war.
- Respond to the Ignite Interview, featuring Ed Boanas.
- Understand how texts reflect the historical context in which they are written.
- Explore the impact and aim of recruitment posters.
- Understand how patriotism can be conveyed through poetry.

2 At the Front	**3 Keeping a Diary**	**4 Class War**
• Explore how language choices and literary features can create a powerful effect. • Consider the sound as well as associations of words. • Understand the effect of present participles.	• Appreciate the use of editing skills in order to make a text clear, informative and interesting for the reader. • Explore and compare diary extracts. • Understand the effectiveness of correct punctuation.	• Explore the layers of meaning in a poem, identifying euphemisms and irony. • Consider and discuss suitable visuals to accompany a poem.
5 Revealing Character	**6 Painting the War**	**7 Rhythms of War**
• Explore how characterization can reinforce the theme of a poem. • Understand the impact of vocabulary and descriptions. • Consider the viewpoint of the poet.	• Plan and draft a poem based on the mood and atmosphere created in a painting. • Explore how tone, mood and atmosphere can be created visually and through words. • Experiment with imagery, vocabulary and sound in a new poem.	• Explore how patterns of language and sound can reinforce the theme of a poem. • Consider the effect of rhythm in 'The Charge of the Light Brigade'. • Perform the poem, using repetition and rhythm to full effect.
8 Shaping the Message	**9 Aftermath**	**10 Assessment**
• Understand how the structure of a poem helps to convey its meaning. • Explore the succinct structure of haiku. • Consider the role of questions in the structure of a poem.	• Consider the effect of rhyme and imagery. • Explore imagery in a wartime novel. • Understand the use of personification in a poem.	• Student Book: Read, assess and select a war poem for display and illustration. • Kerboodle: Read the poem 'War Girls' by Jessie Pope and debate the statement: 'War is no place for a woman?'

Preparing to teach

Refresh your knowledge

You might find it helpful to refer to the following key points when planning your teaching of this unit.

- For millennia, poets have used poetry to record and describe episodes of human conflict, including: tribal battles, sieges, personal quests and vendettas, national and international wars. From the ancient epics of 'Gilgamesh' (18th century BC) and the 'Iliad' (8th century BC), through the world wars of the 20th century, up to and including present-day conflicts, poetry has been a popular form in which to express the trauma, hopes, triumphs, anguish, violence and devastation of war.

- Poetry has sometimes been used by governments as a form of propaganda – to urge men to enlist, to stir up patriotism, and to celebrate victories. However, poetry has also been used by individuals to record their personal experiences of war, to reflect on their role and responsibility, and even to question the rationale for war.

- Poetry can take a wide range of forms, including: free verse, haiku, sonnet, limerick, quatrain, couplet, lyric, ballad, narrative and poetic prose.

- Poetic devices can also be referred to as poetic techniques or poetic conventions, and include: alliteration, assonance, imagery, repetition, rhyme, rhythm and wordplay. Imagery is an umbrella term, including similes, metaphors and personification.

Links and further reading

- www.firstworldwar.com is a comprehensive website that can be used to research the First World War in preparation for teaching the poems of Brooke, Owen and Sassoon.

- The National Association for the Teaching of English (www.nate.org.uk) publishes a variety of resources to support poetry teaching, including *Grammar for Writing: Poetry* by Debra Myhill.

- The English and Media Centre at www.englishandmedia.co.uk produces a variety of downloadable resources, as well as print-based items. Among the most useful for poetry teaching is *The Poetry Book KS3 Series*.

- www.poetryarchive.org offers more poems from and information about poets whose work is included in this unit, such as Siegfried Sassoon, Alfred Lord Tennyson and Simon Armitage.

- www.warpoetry.co.uk contains a wide variety of war poetry, including poems written about more-recent conflicts in Vietnam, Iraq, Afghanistan, Kosovo, and Northern Ireland.

- Recommended sources of poetry for students' independent reading: *Heroes: 100 Poems from the New Generation of War Poets*, edited by John Jeffcock; *Poems of the Great War: 1914–1918*, Penguin Twentieth Century Classics; *101 Poems Against War*, edited by Matthew Hollis and Paul Keegan; *We Are the Dead: Poems and Paintings from the Great War, 1914–1918*, compiled by David Roberts.

- Recommended prose works for students' independent reading: *All Quiet on the Western Front* by Erich Maria Remarque; *A Very Unimportant Officer: Life and Death on the Somme and at Passchendaele* by Captain Alexander Stewart.

Please note that OUP is not responsible for third-party content. Although all links were correct at the time of publication, the content and location of this material may change.

Planning guidance and teaching tips

Think about how you can make the materials relevant to your students and responsive to their needs. Some suggested approaches to address key areas are provided below.

- Poetry is a genre that some students find difficult and feel has little relevance to their lives. However, it is worth pointing out that, in times of great stress or emotion, many people still turn to poetry – whether in the form of religious texts, song lyrics, or personal poetic reflections. Thus, in wartime, many people write poems to express their feelings and recount their experiences.

- Give students time and space to talk about and reflect on their reading. Creating opportunities for them to discuss and share ideas about a text purposefully may help to engage **more-reluctant readers** with negative attitudes towards reading.

- Before they embark on any detailed analysis, ensure that students have sufficient **background information** about the context in which poems were written. Students' knowledge of history and geography may need refreshing accordingly.

- **Interpretation through performance.** Transforming the text in some way will require students to undertake some interpretation of the original. When poems are performed, the attention to pace, tone, feeling and movement can engage students both personally and intellectually. Activities can include reading aloud, paired or choric reading, kinaesthetic embodying of the poem (through tableaux, for example), visual recreations such as collage, or making video films to accompany the poems.

- Understanding individual poems is the main focus of study in this unit. However, **comparing** or **cross-referencing** can help students to appreciate underlying trends and highlight differences of approach. This skill is required from students at GCSE, so some early exposure at Key Stage 3 might be of value.

- Encourage **EAL** students to find poems in their own languages to share in translation with the rest of the class. A positive exercise would be for such students to read a poem aloud in their own language and then to explain or translate it themselves. Explore poetry from a range of international poets to promote inclusivity.

- Provide opportunities for students to experience live poetry. Many poets are available to visit schools and they can motivate students of all abilities to appreciate poetry and have a go at writing their own.

- Provide appropriate **differentiated** support for students' reading and writing through the use of the Kerboodle resources. There are skills-based resources that link to this unit. Ensure an appropriate level of challenge for **gifted and talented** students, for example by encouraging more-confident readers to explore other war poems of their choice and to experiment in their writing, using poetic devices.

- Refer to the **Grammar Reference Guide** on Kerboodle for definitions and exemplars of the specific grammar and punctuation terms covered in this unit. Kerboodle also provides **SPAG interactives** to help improve the technical accuracy of students' reading and writing, and the application of grammar in context. You can assign specific SPAG interactives to individual students or groups of students according to their needs.

Lesson focus

Why are we teaching this?

This introductory lesson offers an opportunity for students to begin thinking about the theme of war in general and the start of the First World War in particular. It looks at how recruitment posters and poetry reflected the attitudes of the time.

What are students learning?

Students will be able to:

● understand how texts reflect the historical context in which they are written.

How you could teach this

A variety of activities and approaches are provided on the right for you to select from and adapt to meet the needs of your students. The Kerboodle lesson player sequence is derived from these suggestions, to act as a starting point for your lesson.

Answers

Answers to Student Book activities, where relevant, can be found on page 63.

Teaching suggestions

Ignition

Ignite English interview

You might like to play Ignite Interview Film 1 to the class. In this film we are introduced to Ed Boanas, infantry officer, and his thoughts about war and war writing.

Resources
Kerboodle: 2 Ignite Interview Ed Boanas Film 1

Exploring concepts

Refer to the charity Help for Heroes, which supports service people who have been affected by combat. Ask students to discuss in pairs what they understand by the term 'hero', before writing a definition using no more than 50 words.

Activate prior learning

As a follow-up to Activities 1 and 2 in the Student Book, ask students to volunteer what they already know about the First World War in particular.

Resources
Student Book 2: Activities 1 and 2, page 33

Exploration

Messages in posters

Before asking students to tackle Activities 1 and 2 in the Student Book, discuss the three First World War posters on page 34. Ensure that all students understand the subtler messages being displayed in each poster, as well as the overt ones. The 'Recruitment posters' image gallery on Kerboodle provides some additional posters for discussion and evaluation.

Resources
Student Book 2: Activities 1 and 2, page 34

Kerboodle: 2.1 Recruitment posters

Role play

Ask students, working in small groups, to role-play a family discussion in which a young man wants to enlist in the army during the First World War. His father is proud and encourages him, but his mother is horrified and tries to persuade him not to.

War debate

Ask students, working in pairs or small groups, to adopt opposing points of view in response to the statement: 'It is always wrong for countries to go to war'. The 'War debate' worksheet on Kerboodle will support this activity.

Resources
Kerboodle: 2.1 War debate

and guidance

Consolidation

Modern military recruitment

Ask students to research current military recruitment advertisements. Encourage them to identify how the messages being used are similar to/different from those used in the First World War. A big difference in today's approach is that military advertisements tend to use exciting videos, rather than posters, and appeal less to patriotism and more to a sense of adventure.

Patriotism

Ensure that all students understand clearly the meaning of the word 'patriotic' before they read Brooke's 'The Soldier' on page 35 of the Student Book and address Activities 3 and 4. They might also benefit from some general discussion about the poem – in particular, the idealistic portrayal of 'England'.

Resources
Student Book 2: Activities 3 and 4, page 35

Performing 'The Soldier'

Ask students, working in groups of three or four, to prepare a recital of 'The Soldier'. Encourage them to decide how to divide up the poem between them, what to emphasize, and how to use tone, pace and volume to enhance the meaning.

'Drummer Hodge'

Ask higher-attaining students to compare Hardy's poem 'Drummer Hodge' (on Kerboodle) with Brooke's 'The Soldier'. You could steer them to think about the presentation of the two characters, the attitudes toward them that each poem sets up, and each poet's views about dying for one's country.

Resources
Kerboodle: 2.1 'Drummer Hodge' by Thomas Hardy

Recital of 'The Soldier'

If you used the Exploration activity that prepared groups of students for a recital of 'The Soldier', you could ask several groups to recite the poem now. The rest of the class could then comment on how effectively the poem's message has been conveyed by each group.

Viewpoint

Ask students whether they think Brooke's poem 'The Soldier', or one of the posters on page 34, would be a more persuasive recruitment tool at the beginning of the First World War. They should explain the reasoning behind their opinions.

The impact of poetic devices

Building on their understanding of alliteration, rhyme, repetition and assonance, ask students what effects these poetic devices create in 'The Soldier'.

Extra Time

Ask students to research more about Rupert Brooke (his life and works). Say that they should find out at least four facts about his life and choose another of his poems about the First World War.

🔗 Weblink   🖥 Presentation   🖱 Interactive activity   **45**

Lesson focus

Why are we teaching this?

This unit focuses on Wilfred Owen's poem 'The Sentry' – tracing its origin from an actual incident recounted in a letter to his mother. It gives students an opportunity to explore how the poet uses language and literary features to give his poem impact and power – relaying a sense of horror, violence and the extreme suffering of injured soldiers and those who were responsible for them.

What are students learning?

Students will be able to:

- explore how language choices and literary features can create a powerful effect.

How you could teach this

A variety of activities and approaches are provided on the right for you to select from and adapt to meet the needs of your students. The Kerboodle lesson player sequence is derived from these suggestions, to act as a starting point for your lesson.

Answers

Answers to Student Book activities, where relevant, can be found on page 63.

Teaching suggestions

Ignition

Key words

Read out the following key words from Owen's poem 'The Sentry' – asking students to guess what the poem is about: 'whizz-bang', 'blast', 'mud', 'shrieking', 'stretcher', 'blind', 'flame', 'body'.

Revise direct speech

Show the 'Revising direct speech' presentation on Kerboodle. Explain that the text extract on the first screen of the presentation contains direct speech but lacks most of its punctuation. Ask students to suggest the correct punctuation and remind them to think also about the use of capital letters. The second screen contains the original punctuated version of the text.

Resources
Kerboodle: 2.2 Revising direct speech

Simile challenge

Challenge students to think of three similes to describe an aspect of life in the trenches during the First World War. Remind them that similes contain the words 'like' or 'as ... as'.

Exploration

Sequencing activity

Give out copies of the 'Sequencing activity' worksheet on Kerboodle. Ask students, working in pairs, to discuss and re-order lines 2-10 of 'The Sentry' to create a coherent meaning. Once the sequencing activity has been completed, and feedback taken to ensure that the order is correct, ask students to complete the remaining activities on the worksheet, either individually or with their partner.

Resources
Kerboodle: 2.2 Sequencing activity

Shared reading

Read the letter extract and poem by Wilfred Owen on page 36 of the Student Book – discussing the real-life event and its transformation into a poem. Focus on the effect of the direct speech in bringing a sense of drama, panic and immediacy to the reader. Encourage students to express their views about the narrator.

Resources
Student Book 2: Activities 1–3, page 37

Planning tableaux

Ask students, working in small groups, to devise a series of tableaux to illustrate scenes or images selected from 'The Sentry'.

and guidance

Consolidation

Recording poetry

If you have suitable recording equipment available, ask students to record their own recitals of 'The Sentry', making sure that their tone is appropriate to the content.

Resources
Recording equipment

An excellent recital of 'The Sentry' by Kenneth Branagh is available on the Internet.

Onomatopoeia and simile

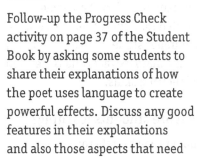

Check students' understanding of onomatopoeia and explore its use in 'The Sentry', including the effect it creates. Also ask students to identify the simile in the poem and discuss the image it creates.

Resources
Student Book 2: Activities 4 and 5, page 37

Ignite English interview

You might like to play Ignite Interview Film 3 to the class, in which Ed Boanas discusses the 100th anniversary of the start of the First World War.

Resources
Kerboodle: 2 Ignite Interview Ed Boanas Film 3

Exploring 'In Memoriam'

Give students copies of the 'In Memoriam' worksheet on Kerboodle. Explain that it uses the concept of a letter from a commanding officer to a father about the death of his son. Ask students to write a diary extract by the same narrator explaining how he felt.

Resources
Kerboodle: 2.2 'In Memoriam' by Ewart Alan Mackintosh

Progress Check

Some students might benefit from the additional guidance provided on the 'Progress Check guidance' worksheet when writing and assessing an explanation of how Owen uses language to create powerful effects in the extract from 'The Sentry' on page 36 of the Student Book.

Resources
Kerboodle: 2.2 Progress Check guidance

Sharing the Progress Check

Follow-up the Progress Check activity on page 37 of the Student Book by asking some students to share their explanations of how the poet uses language to create powerful effects. Discuss any good features in their explanations and also those aspects that need further development.

Resources
Kerboodle: 2.2 Progress Check guidance

Knowledge gained

Ask students to compose a 140-character tweet to explain three things they have learned in this lesson.

Performing tableaux

If you used the 'Planning tableaux' Exploration activity, you could now invite several groups to demonstrate their tableaux – asking the audience to guess which parts of the poem they are illustrating.

Extra Time

Ask students to research 'Dulce et Decorum Est', one of Wilfred Owen's most famous poems. Point out that at the end it states 'The old Lie'. Ask them to decide what the lie is.

Lesson focus

Why are we teaching this?

Most war poems draw from direct experience. In many cases, diaries or letters describe events that later become the subject of poems. Diaries were often used by their writers as a means of working through difficult experiences, rather than being intended for publication. This lesson encourages students to look carefully at some diary extracts and to develop their editing skills.

What are students learning?

Students will be able to:

● appreciate the use of editing skills in order to make a text clear, informative and interesting for a reader.

How you could teach this

A variety of activities and approaches are provided on the right for you to select from and adapt to meet the needs of your students. The Kerboodle lesson player sequence is derived from these suggestions, to act as a starting point for your lesson.

Answers

Answers to Student Book activities, where relevant, can be found on page 63.

Teaching suggestions

Ignition

Genre recognition

Use one of the weblinks below to display a diary extract from the First World War. Ask students to identify the writing genre. Encourage them to explain how they recognized it (drawing out features such as the date, use of the first person and recount style.)

Resources
Weblinks:
www.gutenberg.org/files/18910/18910-h/18910-h.htm#II

www.firstworldwar.com/diaries/index.htm

Editing punctuation

Ask students to discuss which punctuation options are correct in the 'Punctuation' interactive activity on Kerboodle and encourage them to explain their choices.

Resources
Kerboodle: 2.3 Punctuation

Blackadder in the trenches

Play the video clip detailed below. Explain that behind the humour of Blackadder was a lot of truth about the First World War. Point out that many people use humour to disguise other emotions.

Resources
Find the video clip on the Internet from the BBC series *Blackadder Goes Forth*, based in the First World War trenches, entitled 'Good Luck Everybody'.

Exploration

Humour

Ask students to read the two diary extracts on page 38 of the Student Book. Then, in response to Activity 1, discuss Captain Stewart's use of humour – in particular, his use of irony in the final sentence.

Resources
Student Book 2: Activity 1, page 38

Colons and semi-colons

In response to Activity 2 in the Student Book, encourage students to identify the use of a colon and semi-colons in the two diary entries. If necessary, refresh their understanding by using the relevant Grammar Reference Guide sections on Kerboodle.

Resources
Student Book 2: Activity 2, page 38

Kerboodle: Grammar Reference Guide (colons and semi-colons)

Improving impact

Use the 'Editing to improve impact' worksheet on Kerboodle to introduce some editing techniques and give students the opportunity to practise: choosing more-interesting nouns and verbs, adding detail with powerful adverbs or adjectives, and changing the word order.

Resources
Kerboodle: 2.3 Editing to improve impact

and guidance

Consolidation

Punctuating a diary extract

Display the *unpunctuated* diary extract from the presentation on Kerboodle. Explore with students which possible forms of punctuation could be used to make the extract's sense clearer (as well as the use of capital letters). Then display the version of the same extract with its original punctuation in place. Emphasize that there are often several possible ways to punctuate sentences.

Resources
Kerboodle: 2.3 Punctuating a diary extract

Editing a diary extract

Give students the spaced-out worksheet version of Fred's diary extract from page 39 of the Student Book, to assist them with editing and annotating the extract in response to Activity 3. Encourage higher-attaining students to list additional questions to ask Fred.

Resources
Student Book 2: Activity 3, page 39

Kerboodle: 2.3 Fred's diary extract

Write a diary extract

Use the weblinks below to display a few more diary extracts from the Internet. Then ask students to imagine that they are a soldier or nurse in the First World War and to write a suitable diary extract. Remind them to think about writing style as well as content.

Resources
Weblinks:
www.gutenberg.org/files/18910/18910-h/18910-h.htm#II

www.firstworldwar.com/diaries/index.htm

Comic postcards

Display the 'Comic postcards' image gallery of First World War comic postcards by Bruce Bairnsfather on Kerboodle. Encourage students to discuss why they think these postcard images became so popular.

Resources
Kerboodle: 2.3 Comic postcards

Punctuation recap

Challenge students to write two sentences – one with a colon and one with a semi-colon. Share and assess.

Peer-marking

Ask students to either swap the diary extract worksheets they edited for Activity 3 with a partner, or share as a class. Identify two positive editorial changes and one area for improvement in each case.

Role of humour in wartime

Ask students to use evidence from this lesson to explain the importance of humour during the First World War.

Extra Time

Ask students to research information about *The Diary of a Young Girl* by Anne Frank, written during the Second World War. Encourage them to read the whole diary.

Lesson focus

Why are we teaching this?

In this lesson, students will be introduced to the work of a significant author from English literary heritage. They will undertake a careful reading of one of Sassoon's poems, and then consolidate their understanding by completing a textual transformation – converting ideas in the poem into a visual format.

What are students learning?

Students will be able to:

- explore the layers of meaning in a poem, identifying euphemisms and irony.

How you could teach this

A variety of activities and approaches are provided on the right for you to select from and adapt to meet the needs of your students. The Kerboodle lesson player sequence is derived from these suggestions, to act as a starting point for your lesson.

Answers

Answers to Student Book activities, where relevant, can be found on page 63.

Teaching suggestions

Ignition

Contextual referencing

Ask students about any local war memorials they know. Can they describe them? How many names are listed? (There are only eight towns and villages in the UK without World War memorials.)

Memorial

Display the 'Memorial' image from Kerboodle as students come into the room. This image, of the National Memorial Arboretum in Staffordshire, has been deliberately chosen because it is not a classic typical war memorial. Ask students to decide what they think it is memorializing.

Resources
Kerboodle: 2.4 Memorial

Squire

Write 'squire' on the board and ask students what they associate with this historical role. Use their responses to build up a picture of the social hierarchy in rural England in the early 20th century.

Exploration

'Memorial Tablet'

Read and discuss the poem on page 40 of the Student Book before students complete Activities 1a–1e. Confirm their understanding of the terms 'euphemism' and 'irony', by asking them for their own examples.

Discuss why people use euphemisms and then use the 'Euphemisms' interactive activity on Kerboodle to link the examples to their real meaning.

Resources
Student Book 2: Activities 1a–1e, page 41

Kerboodle: 2.4 Euphemisms

Role-play

Ask students, working in small groups, to develop a role-play in which relatives of the dead soldier in 'Memorial Tablet' meet the squire at a village fete. Issue copies of the 'Role-play checklist' on Kerboodle to each group, if required.

Resources
Kerboodle: 2.4 Role-play checklist

Ignite English interview

You might like to play Ignite Interview Film 1 to the class. In this film we are introduced to Ed Boanas and his thoughts about war and war writing.

Resources
Kerboodle: 2 Ignite Interview Ed Boanas Film 1

and guidance

Film sequence

To prompt students with ideas about how they might illustrate the poem 'Memorial Tablet', show the class the 'Images of the First World War' image gallery on Kerboodle. If students don't have easy access to the Internet, they could just sketch or make notes about the type of images they would like to use.

Resources

Student Book 2: Activity 2, page 41

Kerboodle: 2.4 Images of the First World War

Film-making

If feasible, students could use their planned film sequence in response to Activity 2 in the Student Book to make an actual film for display whilst someone recites 'Memorial Tablet'. They could also add music and sound effects to support the tone and mood of the poem.

Resources

Video/film recording equipment

Exploring meaning

Give pairs of students a scenario to recreate, e.g. a commanding officer pinning a medal on a soldier's chest. Say that they have to perform what is being said in one tone of voice, but then say what they are thinking in a different tone of voice.

Progress Check

Students could work in pairs to prepare their recitals of the poem 'Memorial Tablet'. Use the 'Progress Check assessment' worksheet on Kerboodle to help the audience assess each recital.

Resources

Student Book 2: Progress Check, page 41

Kerboodle: 2.4 Progress Check assessment

Creative writing

Ask students to take a news report of a recent conflict and write a poem in the first person, using 'Memorial Tablet' as a model.

Consolidation

Film plans

Share student plans (or actual films) for the visual sequences to accompany a recital of 'Memorial Tablet'. Invite the audience to give two positive comments and one comment highlighting an area for improvement in each case.

Key words

Challenge students, possibly working in pairs, to write definitions of 'euphemism' and 'irony'. Hold a class vote to choose the best definitions.

First person/third person

Ask students to write two sentences – one in the first person and one in the third person. Select a number of students at random to read out their examples. If necessary, make use of the relevant section of the Grammar Reference Guide on Kerboodle to support particular students.

Resources

Kerboodle: Grammar Reference Guide (narrative viewpoint)

Extra Time

Encourage students to visit their local war memorial and write a poem based on the experience.

  Weblink   Presentation   Interactive activity

Lesson focus

Why are we teaching this?

The relatively comfortable lifestyle enjoyed by senior army officers during the First World War contrasted grossly with the suffering of ordinary soldiers at the front. This triggered great resentment, such as that expressed powerfully in Sassoon's poem 'Base Details', which is examined in detail in this lesson – especially through his use of characterization.

What are students learning?

Students will be able to:

- explore how characterization can reinforce the theme of a poem.

How you could teach this

A variety of activities and approaches are provided on the right for you to select from and adapt to meet the needs of your students. The Kerboodle lesson player sequence is derived from these suggestions, to act as a starting point for your lesson.

Answers

Answers to Student Book activities, where relevant, can be found on page 63.

Teaching suggestions

Ignition

Character

Display a painting or photograph of an unusual military character. Ask students what sort of character they think is represented and why they think that.

Resources

Many images can be found on the Internet by searching under 'portraits in uniform' or similar descriptions.

Key words

Display some key words from the poem 'Base Details' on the whiteboard, e.g. 'bald', 'guzzling', 'gulping', 'toddle', 'puffy'. Ask students, working in pairs, to discuss what sort of character these words might apply to.

Title speculation

Write the title of the poem 'Base Details' on the board. Ask students to speculate what it might be about. Draw out different meanings of the word 'base' (the noun meaning starting point, or adjective meaning ignoble).

Exploration

Prose description

Ask students to read the two diary extracts on page 42 of the Student Book and then discuss how Sassoon's judgement of the character is evident through the description.

Resources

Student Book 2: Activity 1a, page 42

Exploring the poem

Ask students, working in pairs, to read 'Base Details' – one student reading the main narrative and the other the direct speech – before completing Activities 2a–2e in the Student Book. As a prelude to tackling the Student Book activities, you could use the 'Character table' worksheet on Kerboodle to allow students to think about and record their first impressions of the 'scarlet Major' after reading the poem.

Resources

Student Book 2: Activities 2a–2e, page 43

Kerboodle: 2.5 Character table

Role-play

Challenge students to play the role of a major, as described by Sassoon, in a short scene of their choice. Ask them to focus on attitude, voice, tone, movement, accent, and gestures. All should convey something about the character.

and guidance

Writing alternative speech

Ask higher-attaining students to rewrite the direct speech in 'Base Details', using alternative words but retaining the characterization, rhythm and rhyme.

Character presentation in film

Show students the trailers for one or more war films. Explore the techniques used by the film-makers and editors to present the main characters.

Resources
Film trailers can be found on the Internet for war films such as *Saving Private Ryan*, *The Green Berets*, *Pearl Harbor*.

Casting director

Ask students, if a film were to be based on Sassoon's poem 'Base Details', what sort of actor they would seek for the roles of the major and the narrator. Ask them to write some notes about age, physique, appearance and character, rather than just suggesting the names of particular actors.

Consolidation

Assess role-plays

If you chose to use the 'Role-play' Exploration activity, invite some students to perform their role-plays now. Encourage constructive comments from the audience about what they did well and which areas could be improved upon.

Alternative direct speech

Ask for volunteers to share the alternative direct speech they wrote. Highlight appropriate capture of character through word choice, expression and accent.

Image comparison

Ask students how they would summarize visually the content of 'Base Details', using two contrasting images. What would feature in each image and how would they differ? Which single word would they choose to describe each image?

Extra Time

Ask students to research some more poems by Siegfried Sassoon – selecting their favourite to read in class and explaining why they like it.

Lesson focus

Why are we teaching this?

Painting and poetry have much in common. They each take a particular episode or incident and render it in a certain mood or tone. In this lesson, students will consider the parallels between the two art forms, and then use a painting as a jumping-off point for their own creative writing.

What are students learning?

Students will be able to:

- plan and draft a poem based on the mood and atmosphere created in a painting.

How you could teach this

A variety of activities and approaches are provided on the right for you to select from and adapt to meet the needs of your students. The Kerboodle lesson player sequence is derived from these suggestions, to act as a starting point for your lesson.

Teaching suggestions

Ignition

Anchoring meaning

Show the class a war painting and ask students to write a one-sentence caption for it. Say that they should concentrate on capturing the mood of the work.

Resources

Search for 'war paintings' on the Internet and select one for display.

Paired discussion

Ask students to discuss in pairs whether they think a painting of war can ever be as powerful as a photograph of war.

Word generator

Display a war painting, which could be the same as or different to the one used above. Give students one minute to note down as many adjectives as they can to describe it – with the aim of using as many unusual words as possible. Give one point for each unique (appropriate) adjective. The student with the most points wins.

Resources

Search for 'war paintings' on the Internet and select one for display.

Exploration

Background information

Before looking in detail at the two paintings in the Student Book, you might want to use the 'Fact sheet' presentation on Kerboodle to give students some background information about Otto Dix and Paul Nash.

Resources

Kerboodle: 2.6 Fact sheet: Otto Dix and Paul Nash

Reading the paintings

Display the image gallery from Kerboodle, which provides large versions of the two paintings from pages 44 and 45 of the Student Book. Then ask students to complete Activities 1a–1f in the Student Book and share responses as a class. Encourage discussion and a variety of interpretations and viewpoints.

Resources

Student Book 2: Activities 1a–1f, page 44

Kerboodle: 2.6 Student Book paintings

Role-play

Ask students to devise a role-play based on one or more of the figures from the paintings on pages 44 and 45 of the Student Book. Use the 'Role-play checklist' on Kerboodle to help if necessary.

Resources

Kerboodle: 2.6 Role-play checklist

Answers

Answers to Student Book activities, where relevant, can be found on page 63.

and guidance

Consolidation

Writing monologue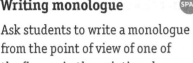

Ask students to write a monologue from the point of view of one of the figures in the paintings by Nash or Dix. Remind them to write in the first person. If necessary, use the relevant section of the Grammar Reference Guide on Kerboodle to reinforce knowledge about narrative viewpoint.

Resources
Kerboodle: Grammar Reference Guide (narrative viewpoint)

Writing a poem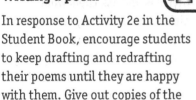

In response to Activity 2e in the Student Book, encourage students to keep drafting and redrafting their poems until they are happy with them. Give out copies of the 'Guidance for writing a poem' worksheet on Kerboodle to help students where necessary.

Resources
Student Book 2: Activities 2a–2e, page 45

Kerboodle: 2.6 Guidance for writing a poem

Writing from film

The evocative film compilation, *WW1 Combat in Colour 1914–1918*, uses rare colour archive images and music to chart the history of the First World War. You could ask students to write a poem inspired by this moving montage.

Resources
Enter 'WW1 Combat in Colour 1914–1918 sonicbomb.com' into a search engine to access the clip.

Picture composition

In response to the Extra Time activity on page 45 of the Student Book, encourage a discussion about which painting is the most modern in style. Higher-attaining students could use the 'Picture-composition analysis' worksheet on Kerboodle to go into more depth.

Resources
Student Book 2: Extra Time activity, page 45

Kerboodle: 2.6 Picture-composition analysis

Peer assessment

Ask each student to swap their draft poem from Activity 2 in the Student Book with a partner. Each one should then feed back two strengths and one point for development in response to their partner's poem.

Evaluation

Ask students to write a 140-character tweet outlining what they have learned in this lesson.

Share monologues

If you chose to use the 'Writing monologue' Exploration activity, invite some students to read out their monologues. Ask the audience to suggest which character in which picture is 'speaking', and also explain why they think that.

Extra Time

Ask students, if they saw both Student Book paintings in a gallery and knew nothing about them, which one they think would be the most modern. Ask them to explain their answers carefully.

  Weblink   Presentation   Interactive activity

Lesson focus

Why are we teaching this?

Laurence Ferlinghetti has said that poetry should be 'heard not read'. The sound of a poem is of huge significance. This lesson will increase students' awareness of how poets use vocabulary to create a variety of sound effects and, in particular, rhythm.

What are students learning?

Students will be able to:

● explore how patterns of language and sound can reinforce the theme of a poem.

How you could teach this

A variety of activities and approaches are provided on the right for you to select from and adapt to meet the needs of your students. The Kerboodle lesson player sequence is derived from these suggestions, to act as a starting point for your lesson.

Answers

Answers to Student Book activities, where relevant, can be found on page 63.

Teaching suggestions

Ignition

Tuning in to rhythm

Play a piece of music and encourage students to clap out the underlying rhythm. Then ask them to clap every other beat or double up the time by clapping. Link the notion of rhythm in music with poetry.

Nursery rhymes

Ask students, working in pairs, to share any nursery rhymes or songs they still remember from when they were very young. Encourage them to say/sing them.

Drummers

Play a clip from a performance by the Drummers of Burundi and initiate a discussion about drumming in general, its historical uses, and general appeal to our love of rhythm.

Resources
Find video clips of the Drummers of Burundi on the Internet.

Exploration

Limericks

Use the 'Limericks' presentation on Kerboodle to share a number of limericks with the class. Encourage students to count the syllables and tap out the rhythms. Then ask them to write a limerick of their own, obeying the rules of the form.

Resources
Kerboodle: 2.7 Limericks

Conveying mood with rhythm

Play students a variety of drum rhythms and ask them what different moods they convey. Contrast rousing marching military drums with anticipatory drum rolls and dance music of bongos and congas.

Patterns of sound

Ask students to complete Activities 1a–1c in the Student Book without giving them any background information. Make sure that they explore the sound effects created in the extract.

Resources
Student Book 2: Activities 1a–1c, page 46

and guidance

Consolidation

'The Charge of the Light Brigade'

Use 'The Charge of the Light Brigade' worksheet on Kerboodle to provide students with the complete text of Tennyson's poem, plus some contextual information about it.

Resources

Kerboodle: 2.7 'The Charge of the Light Brigade' by Tennyson

'Fifteen Million Plastic Bags'

As a Stretch activity, you could give higher-attaining students the 'Fifteen Million Plastic Bags' worksheet on Kerboodle, which contains the complete text of the Cold War poem by Adrian Mitchell, plus some contextual information to support the accompanying activities.

Resources

Kerboodle: 2.7 'Fifteen Million Plastic Bags' by A. Mitchell

Ignite English interview

You might like to play Ignite Interview Film 2 to the class, in which Ed Boanas discusses communication through the written and spoken word.

Resources

Kerboodle: 2 Ignite Interview Ed Boanas Film 2

Performing verse

In response to Activity 3 in the Student Book, ask students (working in small groups) to develop a performance of 'The Charge of the Light Brigade'. Remind them to consider tone, volume, pace, and whether to divide the narration between them or to perform chorally.

Resources

Student Book 2: Activity 3, page 47

Listening to recital

Recordings from the Internet of 'The Charge of the Light Brigade' may give students some ideas to help them with their own performances.

Resources

Recitals of 'The Charge of the Light Brigade' can be found on the Internet, e.g. by Bransby Williams.

Progress Check

Ask the different groups to perform 'The Charge of the Light Brigade', followed by feedback from the audience. The 'Progress Check assessment' worksheet on Kerboodle provides a detailed checklist for assessment. Make sure that students are aware of areas for improvement as well as areas of achievement.

Resources

Student Book 2: Activity 4, page 47

Kerboodle: 2.7 Progress Check assessment

Recap on sound effects in poetry

Ask students to explain to a partner three techniques that poets use to create sound effects in their work. They should be prepared to give examples of each.

Sharing work

If you chose to use the 'Limericks' Exploration activity, you could now ask volunteers to read out their limericks. The audience should respond by giving them a thumbs up or thumbs down, depending on how well they stuck to a clear rhythm.

Extra Time

Encourage students to find a poem that they particularly like the sound of. They should prepare to read it and explain some of the sound effects that the poet creates.

 Weblink   Presentation   Interactive activity

Lesson focus

Why are we teaching this?

One of the key ways in which we can tell that something is a poem, is by its shape on the page. This shape is constructed out of line lengths and breaks between verses. The structure of a poem enables the poet to make the reader focus on certain words, phrases or lines, and builds up a visual pattern of content. It is very important that students have a clear grasp of this.

What are students learning?

Students will be able to:

- understand how the structure of a poem helps to convey its meaning.

How you could teach this

A variety of activities and approaches are provided on the right for you to select from and adapt to meet the needs of your students. The Kerboodle lesson player sequence is derived from these suggestions, to act as a starting point for your lesson.

Teaching suggestions

Ignition

Shape poems

Display a range of shape poems from the Internet and ask students how the content relates to the physical structure of each poem.

Resources
Use the phrase 'shape poems' to locate suitable examples.

Poetry forms

Sketch the outline shape of various poetic forms on the board, representing: a sonnet, rhyming couplets, narrative poem (no verses), a limerick, a hymn. Challenge students to identify what each could be.

Exploration

Haiku

Before they attempt Activities 1 and 2 in the Student Book, you could show students the haiku examples in the 'Haiku' presentation on Kerboodle. Explain that the tight form of haiku means that the poet has to condense their ideas very succinctly, choosing vocabulary with great care.

Resources
Student Book 2: Activities 1 and 2, page 48

Kerboodle: 2.8 Haiku

Writing a haiku

Lower-attaining students might benefit from using the 'Haiku writing support' worksheet on Kerboodle to help them complete Activity 3 in the Student Book.

Resources
Student Book 2: Activity 3, page 48

Kerboodle: 2.8 Haiku writing support

'What Were They Like?'

Read the Denise Levertov poem 'What Were They Like?' on page 49 of the Student Book. Ask students to think in particular about the structure of the poem.

Answers

Answers to Student Book activities, where relevant, can be found on page 63.

and guidance

Consolidation

Clerihew

Give students, working in groups, some examples of clerihews from the following weblinks, and then ask them to use the examples to deduce the 'rules' for clerihew writing. After agreeing a class definition, ask students to write a clerihew of their own about someone associated with war, e.g. Napoleon, Joan of Arc.

Resources
Weblinks:
http://www.gigglepoetry.com/poetryclass/clerihew.htm

http://thinks.com/words/clerihew.htm

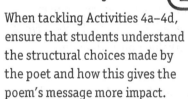

Structural analysis

When tackling Activities 4a–4d, ensure that students understand the structural choices made by the poet and how this gives the poem's message more impact.

Resources
Student Book 2: Activity 4a–4c, page 49

Comparison of images

In response to Activity 4d in the Student Book, ask students to explore how the imagery is built up and how comparisons throw each image into greater relief. Encourage close analysis of vocabulary and connotations of specific words.

Resources
Student Book 2: Activity 4d, page 49

Experimenting with structure

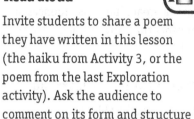

Ask students to write their own short poem, about war or an issue associated with war, using the same question/answer structure as 'What Were They Like?'

Read aloud

Invite students to share a poem they have written in this lesson (the haiku from Activity 3, or the poem from the last Exploration activity). Ask the audience to comment on its form and structure and how it contributes towards the meaning of the poem.

Key terms

Use the 'Poetry' interactive activity on Kerboodle to check students' knowledge about the key terms used in this lesson.

Resources
Kerboodle: 2.8 Poetry

Evaluation

Ask students to write a 140-character tweet explaining what they have learned about poetic form in this lesson.

Extra Time

Encourage students to research more war poetry, choose a poem that they feel has great impact, and learn it (or part of it) by heart to recite to the class.

Lesson focus

Why are we teaching this?

Many poets and authors have expressed their feelings about the long-term consequences of war. Sometimes the devastating effects can be best summed up with the use of imagery, suggesting more far-reaching consequences and concepts than any literal description could.

What are students learning?

Students will be able to:

- consider the effect of rhyme and imagery.

How you could teach this

A variety of activities and approaches are provided on the right for you to select from and adapt to meet the needs of your students. The Kerboodle lesson player sequence is derived from these suggestions, to act as a starting point for your lesson.

Teaching suggestions

Ignition

Rhyming couplets

Display a variety of poetic couplets as students enter the classroom. Ask them to write a couplet of their own about how they feel about their day so far.

Revise metaphor and simile

Ask students to volunteer definitions for and examples of metaphor and simile. Encourage each student to write one metaphor or simile about a friend.

Aftermath

Write 'aftermath' on the board and ask students what this makes them think of. Draw out the meaning: the consequences of a significant, often bad or unpleasant, event.

Exploration

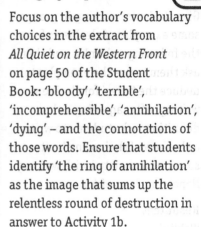

Imagery in prose

Focus on the author's vocabulary choices in the extract from *All Quiet on the Western Front* on page 50 of the Student Book: 'bloody', 'terrible', 'incomprehensible', 'annihilation', 'dying' – and the connotations of those words. Ensure that students identify 'the ring of annihilation' as the image that sums up the relentless round of destruction in answer to Activity 1b.

Resources
Student Book 2: Activities 1a and 1b, page 50

All Quiet on the Western Front

Activities 1a–1c in the Student Book could be extended using the '*All Quiet on the Western Front*' worksheet on Kerboodle.

Resources
Kerboodle: 2.9 *All Quiet on the Western Front*

Ignite English interview

You might like to play Ignite Interview Film 1 to the class. In this film we are introduced to Ed Boanas and his thoughts about war and war writing.

Resources
Kerboodle: 2 Ignite Interview Ed Boanas Film 1

Answers

Answers to Student Book activities, where relevant, can be found on page 63.

and guidance

Images as symbols

Discuss images that are used as symbols, e.g. a dove (peace), a handshake (friendship). Ask students which image is commonly used to symbolize remembrance of soldiers (the poppy). Then ask why they think it is so powerful as an image, and whether they can suggest an alternative. You could reinforce this activity by showing the class the closing scene from the last episode of *Blackadder Goes Forth*, when the battlefield image of slaughter is transformed into a field of poppies.

Resources
You can find the relevant clip of *Blackadder Goes Forth* on the Internet.

'There Will Come Soft Rains'

Before they attempt Activities 2a–2b in the Student Book, read the poem 'There Will Come Soft Rains' with students – checking their understanding of the terms 'personification', 'full rhyme' and 'half rhyme'. Ask students why they think the poet chose to use rhyming couplets to express her ideas.

Resources
Student Book 2: Activities 2a–2b, page 51

Write a poem 'Aftermath'

Additional support for Activity 3 in the Student Book, in terms of vocabulary, ideas and structure, is available in the 'Aftermath support' worksheet on Kerboodle.

Resources
Student Book 2: Activity 3, page 51

Kerboodle: 2.9 'Aftermath' support

Imagist poetry

Use the 'Imagist poetry' worksheet on Kerboodle to introduce higher-attaining students to the Imagist Movement. Encourage them to write their own Imagist poem, using the structure of object–image–development.

Resources
Kerboodle: 2.9 Imagist poetry

Consolidation

Imagery

Ask students how they would define 'imagery'. Work towards a class definition, with examples.

Share and evaluate

Share some students' work and ask for evaluative comments – two identifying areas of strength and one suggesting where more work might be appropriate.

Sharing views

Ask students, working in pairs, to tell each other three things they have learned from this lesson.

Extra Time

Ask students to consider whether they think the natural world will always recover after war. Encourage them to write a paragraph expressing their ideas.

Assessment focus

Why are we assessing this?

Students have completed a unit on the poetry of war. They have encountered a variety of poetry, in terms of form and structure, historical context and thematic content. This assessment focuses on their ability to read, comprehend and analyse a poem chosen from a selection of three. They should complete the written task independently.

What are students demonstrating?

Students will be able to:

- express an informed personal response to a poem.

How to deliver the assessment

Suggestions and guidance on how to set up and prepare your students for the assessment are provided, as well as possible approaches to marking the assessment.

Alternative/additional assessment

There is an alternative end-of-unit assessment available on Kerboodle. This assessment leads to a spoken English outcome and can be used either in addition to or instead of the Student Book end-of-unit assessment.

Resources
Kerboodle: 2.10 Alternative end-of-unit assessment 📄

Assessment suggestions and guidance

Understanding the assessment

Check that students understand the assessment task set. Emphasize that they are being tested on their writing skills.

Resources
Student Book 2: pages 52–55

Reading and planning

Remind students that they will need to choose an appropriate way to plan their work. They should include this plan as part of their assessment.

Completing the assessment

Emphasize that they must complete the task individually, so that an accurate assessment of their achievement can be given.

Timing and writing expectation

Give students one hour (ideally one lesson) and expect between one and two A4 pages.

Marking

You will want to mark this in line with departmental and school marking guidelines. If you wish, you could use the Ignite English marking scales provided on Kerboodle. Using the Ignite English marking scales will help you to identify specific strengths and areas for improvement in an individual student's writing. This may help you to set development targets as well as building a profile of your class as writers.

Refer to the KS3 National Curriculum and Ignite English mapping grids on pages 154–156 of this Teacher Companion to identify other Ignite English units where these writing skills are covered, or ask students to use the SPAG interactives on Kerboodle to address any areas identified for improvement. The Grammar Reference Guide on Kerboodle contains definitions and additional examples of each of the spelling, punctuation and grammar points covered in the interactives, for your reference.

Resources
Kerboodle: 2 Ignite English marking scales 📄

Kerboodle: SPAG interactives 🖱

Kerboodle: Grammar Reference Guide

Student Book answers

Below are the answers to any largely non-subjective Student Book activities contained within this unit.

Lesson 2

2   The words 'whined' and 'sobbed' emphasize his pain and suffering and they create sympathy for him.

3   The narrator does what he can to help but has to get on with other tasks; however, the image of the man returns to haunt him in his dreams.

5   The simile 'huge-bulged like squids' conveys an image of swollen eyeballs that look deformed and grotesque.

Lesson 3

1   Stewart used his sense of humour to cope.

Lesson 4

1a He was pressurised into joining up by his Squire and he died in battle; he hates and blames the Squire for what happened to him; feels his life was wasted.

1b He 'bullied' the young man into joining up and is portrayed as a hypocrite.

1c These euphemisms are another way of saying he died; the first is a powerful and poetic use of language; the second reflects the soldier's ordinary status.

1d 'hell' and 'anguish' are the real face of war' there is nothing 'proud' or 'glorious' about it.

1e This is ironic because the young man would rather be alive; he does not see any 'glory' in dying at war.

Lesson 5

1a Sassoon thinks the Brigadier-General is a hypocrite and he hates him.

1b He was killed when young and did not get to achieve anything in life.

1c Anger and disgust.

2b

Bullet point 1: unfit

Bullet point 2: greedy

Bullet point 3: fat, unhealthy, a ridiculous figure

Bullet point 4: he dies peacefully in his sleep

2c He is upper class and does not really care about the young man.

Lesson 7

1a A cavalry charge under canon fire.

1c He admires their bravery and skill, 'boldly they rode and well'.

Lesson 8

1   The fight for freedom/Won't end 'til we teach children/Love instead of hate

2   Its simple form makes the message more powerful.

4a The first voice stops in verse one when the questions stop in line 9.

4b They come at the end of the sentence.

4c This reflects that asking questions is easy but the answers to such questions are very complicated and so harder and more difficult to explain.

Lesson 9

1a Resigned and despairing.

1b 'The days stand like angels in blue and gold, incomprehensible, above the ring of annihilation'; this conveys Heaven's despair at how man can be so cruel and barbaric.

1c That Nature would once again come to life and renew itself

2a The personification, 'singing', 'woke', 'wear', 'whistling' is used ironically because it is a poem about a happier world without humans.

2b Full rhyme used except for lines 9 and 10 because this emphasizes the main point of the poem.

Unit 3: Appearance and Reality

Unit overview

Why are we teaching this?

This unit explores how the differences between appearance and reality have been used by writers over time for dramatic effect. It also explores how authors, poets and playwrights use a range of literary techniques to develop this theme in ways that illuminate ideas and entertain readers. The unit provides a purposeful context for teaching **critical reading skills** (such as studying **setting**, **plot** and **characterization**) and exploring literary techniques (such as the use of **unreliable narrators**, **puns** and **extended metaphors**).

Students will read and respond to a wide range of fiction, poetry and plays, including extracts from Shakespeare's *Twelfth Night*, poems by T.S. Eliot and William Blake, and fiction from authors such as Lewis Carroll, Anne Fine and Edgar Allan Poe. They have the opportunity to develop a personal response to the texts they read, exploring these through discussion and performance, and applying specific techniques and approaches to their own writing.

What are the learning aims?

By the end of the unit, students will be able to:

- develop a personal response to the texts they read – tracing how the theme of appearance and reality has been used in literature across time in different contexts and forms

- read critically to explore how setting, plot and characterization are established and developed

- explore how specific techniques, such as puns, extended metaphor and unreliable narration, are used to create humour and provide insights.

How will this be assessed?

Key assessment task	Focus for assessment
Student Book: Reading analysis of an extract from *Madame Doubtfire* by Anne Fine.	• Exploring how figurative language and vocabulary are used to present meaning. • Exploring characterization. • Explaining how the writer creates humour in the extract.
Kerboodle: Rehearsing and performing a scene from *Madame Doubtfire*.	• Using tone, intonation and volume to create the role of the character they are playing. • Using body language, movement, silence, stillness and gesture for comic effect. • Bringing out the dramatic irony of the scene through their improvisation and performance.

The end-of-unit assessment on Kerboodle can be used either instead of or in addition to the Student Book end-of-unit assessment.

Note that short Progress Checks also feature in this unit, providing formative assessment opportunities to support students' learning.

Lesson sequence

This is a suggested lesson sequence, but you might choose to alter or add to it to suit your particular teaching needs.

Introducing the unit

1 Writing the Illusion

- Draw on prior knowledge of differences between appearance and reality.
- Respond to the Ignite interview, featuring Debbie Korley.
- Analyse and interpret how character and setting are created.
- Create a set design for a stage adaptation of *The Night Circus* by Erin Morgenstern.
- Write an email to the actors playing the parts of the characters in the scene, drawing on details from the text.

---

2 Unreliable Narrators

- Explore the role of the unreliable narrator in fiction.
- Read extracts from 'The Tell-Tale Heart' by Edgar Allan Poe and *The Boy in the Striped Pyjamas* by John Boyne, looking at how vocabulary and sentence structures are used to suggest an unreliable narrator.
- Discuss the rationale for the use of unreliable narrators.

3 Looking Differently

- Investigate how and why writers use extended metaphors.
- Read extracts from 'The Love Song of J. Alfred Prufrock' by T.S. Eliot and 'A Poison Tree' by William Blake.
- Explore the use of extended metaphors in these poems and use this technique in their own writing.

4 Wordplay and Puns

- Consider how puns and other forms of wordplay can be used to create humour.
- Read and analyse the use of wordplay in two extracts from *Alice's Adventures in Wonderland* by Lewis Carroll.
- Create a comic script of a conversation using puns and wordplay.

---

5 Under the Skin

- Evaluate the way in which folk tales exploit the theme of outward appearance.
- Read and analyse an extract from the Brothers Grimm folk tale 'Bearskin'.
- Plan and continue the story of 'Bearskin' from where the extract leaves off.

6 Deception and Lies

- Explore the ideas and issues around deception and mistaken identity through discussion and improvisation.
- Read a newspaper article about Frédéric Bourdin.
- Improvise a scene where the Barclay family discover that the person they thought was their missing son is actually Frédéric Bourdin.

7 Beneath the Disguise

- Develop, through rehearsal and discussion, a personal response to lines from Shakespeare's *Twelfth Night*.
- Explore different interpretations of the extract through performance.
- Enhance and perfect a final rehearsal of the extract.

---

8 Truth and Nonsense

- Develop an understanding of the role of the fool in *Twelfth Night*.
- Read and analyse two further extracts from *Twelfth Night*, in particular the use of word play by Feste in the scenes.
- Identify the characteristics of a fool, as displayed by Feste in the two extracts.

9 Assessment

- Student Book: Read and analyse an extract from *Madame Doubtfire* by Anne Fine.
- Kerboodle: Rehearse and perform a scene from *Madame Doubtfire*.

Preparing to teach

Refresh your knowledge

You might find it helpful to refer to the following key points when planning your teaching of this unit.

- The difference between outer appearance and inner reality is a popular theme in literature, dating back to the theatre of ancient Greece and Rome, e.g. in the work of playwrights like Menander and Plautus. William Shakespeare explored this theme in his comedies, such as *As You Like It*, *Twelfth Night* and *The Comedy of Errors*, where mistaken identity, deception and disguise are the impetus behind the action.

- In fiction, the 'unreliable narrator' is a technique first named in the mid-20th century, but subsequently identified in classic novels such as Jonathan Swift's *Gulliver's Travels* and Daniel Defoe's *Moll Flanders*. The following classifications are often used to identify different types of unreliable narrator: the Picaro (a narrator who exaggerates events), the Madman (a narrator whose perception of events is impaired by mental illness), the Clown (a narrator who plays with narrative conventions to subvert the reader's expectations), the Naif (a narrator who has a limited insight into the events they describe, e.g. due to their immaturity), the Liar (a narrator who misrepresents events for their own purpose).

- The use of puns and word play is a common feature in Shakespearean plays – often used for comedic effect – and this technique can also be seen in novels such as Lewis Carroll's *Alice's Adventures in Wonderland*, where linguistic word play is used to create surreal imagery and amusing juxtapositions of meaning. As well as creating humour, the use of figurative language (such as simile, metaphor and personification) is also employed in literature to reveal essential truths – providing readers with unexpected insights, as layers of meaning are peeled back.

- The theme of appearance and reality is one that has been explored in many genres – from fantasy and adventure to comedy and mystery – with disguise, deception and mistaken identity often forming a vital part of fictional plots. Folk and fairy tales, such as *Cinderella*, are predicated on the differences between outward appearance and inner truth. Films, TV programmes and contemporary children's fiction, such as *Fifteen Days Without a Head* by Dave Cousins, use cross-dressing as a literary trope for dramatic or comedic effect.

Links and further reading

- The websites of the Globe Theatre (http://www.shakespearesglobe.com/education) and the RSC (http://www.rsc.org.uk/education/) provide a vast array of useful resources and ideas for the teaching of Shakespeare.

- A virtual ebook of Lewis Carroll's original manuscript for *Alice's Adventures Under Ground* (the original version of *Alice's Adventures in Wonderland*) is available from the British Library website: http://www.bl.uk/onlinegallery/ttp/alice/accessible/introduction.html

- Recommendations for students' independent reading include: *Manga Shakespeare: Twelfth Night* by William Shakespeare, Richard Appignanesi and Nana Li; *Selected Tales* by Edgar Allan Poe; *Alice's Adventures in Wonderland* by Lewis Carroll; *The Boy in the Striped Pyjamas* by John Boyne; *Grimm Tales* by Philip Pullman; *Madame Doubtfire* by Anne Fine; *Fifteen Days Without a Head* by Dave Cousins; *Songs of Innocence and Experience* by William Blake; *Stratford Boys* by Jan Mark.

Please note that OUP is not responsible for third-party content. Although all links were correct at the time of publication, the content and location of this material may change.

Planning guidance and teaching tips

Think about how you can make the materials relevant to your students and responsive to their needs. Some suggested approaches to address key areas are provided below.

- Be prepared to work with students with lower reading ages and **EAL** students, in one-to-one and guided-group contexts, to support their reading of the texts included in this unit (especially the extract from *Alice's Adventures in Wonderland* by Lewis Carroll, where the word play and puns might need further explanation).

- Give students time in the classroom to talk about and reflect on their independent reading. Creating opportunities for students to discuss and share ideas about a text can help to engage **more-reluctant readers** and dispel any negative attitudes about reading.

- **Modelling** responses to reading for students would be particularly beneficial in this unit. Developing students' skills in the elements they need to critically respond in writing to the texts they read will help to prepare them for the end-of-unit assessment.

- Refer to the **Grammar Reference Guide** on Kerboodle for definitions and exemplars of specific grammar and punctuation terms, as highlighted by the Literacy Feature icon. Kerboodle also provides **SPAG interactives** to help improve the technical accuracy of students' writing and the application of grammar in context. You can assign specific SPAG interactives to individual students or groups of students according to their needs.

Lesson focus

Why are we teaching this?

Lesson 1 introduces the Appearance and Reality unit, by following up initial work about students' own lying with the analysis of an extract from the novel *The Night Circus* by Erin Morgenstern – using it to explore how character and setting are created in this description of an illusion.

What are students learning?

Students will be able to:

- analyse and interpret how character and setting are created.

How you could teach this

A variety of activities and approaches are provided on the right for you to select from and adapt to meet the needs of your students. The Kerboodle lesson player sequence is derived from these suggestions, to act as a starting point for your lesson.

Teaching suggestions

Ignition

Ignite English interview

You might like to play Ignite Interview Film 1 to the class. In this film we are introduced to Debbie Korley, actress and RSC practitioner, and her thoughts about acting.

Resources

Kerboodle: 3 Ignite Interview Debbie Korley Film 1

Truth and lies

Ask pairs of students to tell each other three new things about themselves – two of which are true and one of which is a lie. Conduct feedback by discussing how easy or difficult it is to identify a lie, and also which techniques students have used to disguise a lie (both in this activity and on previous occasions).

Resources

Student Book 2: Activities 1 and 2, page 57

Reflecting on prior reading or watching

Ask students, working in pairs or small groups, to discuss any books, films or TV programmes that they may have watched or read, which explore the differences between appearance and reality. Encourage them to articulate how the theme was presented and also to discuss what they enjoyed most about these stories.

Exploration

Shared reading

As a prelude to Activity 1 in the Student Book, use shared reading to identify the textual details used by Erin Morgenstern to create the setting in the extract, e.g. 'a line of black iron sconces along the rounded wall', 'a ring of plain wooden chairs ... only about twenty of them, in two staggered rows', 'Bailey chooses a seat in the inside row, across from the entrance', etc. Encourage students to read closely – drawing details from different parts of the text to build a picture of the setting.

Resources

Student Book 2: Activity 1, page 58

Setting the stage

Use the 'Designing the set' worksheet on Kerboodle to help students to complete Activity 1 in the Student Book. Remind them of the importance of referring to the text to justify their set-design choices.

Resources

Student Book 2: Activity 1, page 58

Kerboodle: 3.1 Designing the set

Answers

Answers to Student Book activities, where relevant, can be found on page 85.

and guidance

Consolidation

Creating the illusion

Challenge higher-achieving students to brainstorm possible ways in which the illusions of the disappearing entrance and the chair catching fire could be achieved. You could support this activity by using the weblink below to show a newspaper article that discusses possible solutions to the tricks performed by Dynamo (a television magician and illusionist). Ask students to write a set of instructions explaining how to perform one of these illusions.

Resources
Student Book 2: Stretch Activity 1, page 58

Weblink: http://www.telegraph.co.uk/news/uknews/10140245/Are-these-the-secrets-behind-Dynamos-greatest-tricks.html

Advertising the illusion

Display the 'Magic show adverts' image gallery on Kerboodle, which illustrates various poster adverts for magic shows and illusionists. Explore the techniques used to encourage readers to attend the shows (e.g. image, symbols, colour, tagline, etc.) and discuss their effectiveness. Ask students to create their own poster advertising the illusionist's show in the Student Book extract.

Resources
Kerboodle: 3.1 Magic show adverts

Reviewing the show

Writing in role as Bailey, ask students to review the illusionist's show. Encourage them to refer to details from the text when describing the illusions performed, and also to consider how the vocabulary they choose can help to articulate Bailey's thoughts and feelings about the show he has seen.

Continuing the story

Challenge students to write the next section of the story. Discuss what other illusions the illusionist could perform – and how the audience might react to them. Encourage them to write in the same style as Erin Morgenstern, using adverbs, adjectives and similes to describe the illusionist's actions and the impressions they create.

Character emails

Ask students to respond to Activity 3 in the Student Book by writing an email to the actors playing the parts of Bailey and the illusionist – giving advice on how they should play these parts. Model how to refer to details from the Student Book extract to support the advice being given, e.g. 'When you are performing the burning chair trick, ensure that you show how in control you are by keeping your movements calm and unhurried, as in "she calmly unbuttons her coat".'

Resources
Student Book 2: Activity 3, page 59

Staging the scene

Get students to work in small groups to create a performance of the scene. Encourage them to use a range of dramatic techniques, such as tableaux, to create a sense of the spectacle of the illusion through the characters' reactions.

Setting tips

Ask students to create a list of three tips for creating an effective setting. Encourage them to link their tips to examples from their reading.

Extra Time

Encourage students to research how to perform their own illusion or magic trick.

Lesson focus

Why are we teaching this?

This lesson challenges students' expectations about the reliability of first-person narratives – introducing the concept of the unreliable narrator. Through reading and analysing extracts from Edgar Allan Poe's short story 'The Tell-Tale Heart', as well as *The Boy in the Striped Pyjamas* by John Boyne, students explore the different ways in which an unreliable narrator can be created – and also discuss the reasons why writers use this technique.

What are students learning?

Students will be able to:

- explore the role of the unreliable narrator in fiction.

How you could teach this

A variety of activities and approaches are provided on the right for you to select from and adapt to meet the needs of your students. The Kerboodle lesson player sequence is derived from these suggestions, to act as a starting point for your lesson.

Answers

Answers to Student Book activities, where relevant, can be found on page 85.

Teaching suggestions

Ignition

Unreliable narrator

Show 'The unreliable narrator' presentation on Kerboodle and ask questions to check students' understanding of the technique.

Resources
Kerboodle: 3.2 The unreliable narrator

First-person narratives

Ask students to identify the first-person narrative extracts in the 'First-person narratives' interactive activity on Kerboodle. Discuss how the use of pronouns and nouns is an indicator.

Resources
Kerboodle: 3.2 First-person narratives

Misleading the reader

Ask students to write an estate agent's description of their bedroom. Encourage them to exaggerate things, omit inconvenient details, and even lie to try to create the most-attractive description. Feed back by discussing the techniques they used to try to mislead the reader.

Exploration

Shared reading

Support Activity 1a in the Student Book by using shared reading of the extract on page 61 to identify those textual details that suggest the narrator might be unreliable, e.g. his direct address to the reader ('Why will you say that I am mad?') and describing his hearing as being impossibly acute ('I heard all things in the heaven and in the earth'). Explore with students what inferences can be made about the narrator from the textual details identified.

Resources
Student Book 2: Activity 1a, page 60

Sentence analysis

Ask students to use the 'Poe's techniques' worksheet on Kerboodle to explore how Edgar Allan Poe's choice of sentence structure and use of punctuation suggests that the narrator is unreliable.

Resources
Student Book 1: Activity 1b, page 60

Kerboodle: 3.2 Poe's techniques

and guidance

Exploration

Ignite English interview

You might like to play Ignite Interview Film 1 to the class. In this film we are introduced to Debbie Korley and her thoughts about acting.

Resources
Kerboodle: 3 Ignite Interview Debbie Korley Film 1

Class discussion

You could expand Activity 2 in the Student Book by asking students to read all of 'The Tell-Tale Heart' (provided on Kerboodle) before discussing possible reasons why Edgar Allan Poe chose a first-person narrative to tell the story. Encourage them to consider the story's genre and its implications on the author's narrative choice.

Resources
Student Book 2: Activity 2, page 60

Kerboodle: 3.2 'The Tell-Tale Heart'

Hot-seating the narrator

Ask a student to work in role as the narrator of 'The Tell-Tale Heart'. Hot-seat this character, with other students asking questions to find out more about his actions and the reasons for carrying out the murder. Encourage the student working in role as the narrator to use tone, intonation, silence, stillness and action to suggest the narrator's madness.

Ignition

Model reading

Support Activity 3 in the Student Book by model reading the extract from *The Boy in the Striped Pyjamas* on page 63. Identify some textual details which suggest that Bruno doesn't fully understand what is happening in the concentration camp. For example, he describes the prisoners as 'pyjama people', which indicates that he isn't aware that they are being kept prisoner. He also doesn't seem aware that when the prisoners 'sometimes … fell to the ground … didn't even get up' this means that they have probably died.

Resources
Student Book 2: Activity 3, page 62

Hot-seating Bruno

As a prelude to Activity 4 in the Student Book, ask a student to work in role as Bruno. Hot-seat this character, with other students asking questions to find out how much he knows about the reality of life in the concentration camp. Encourage the student working in role as Bruno to give answers that emphasize his naivety and lack of understanding.

Resources
Student Book 2: Activity 4, page 62

Consolidation

Progress Check

As a Stretch activity, ask students to write a paragraph explaining what an unreliable narrator is – giving examples from the extracts they have read to support their explanation.

More unreliable narrators

Using the 'More unreliable narrators' worksheet on Kerboodle, ask students to identify the different types of unreliable narrator being exemplified, as well as the textual details that suggest their narration is unreliable.

Resources
Kerboodle: 3.2 More unreliable narrators

Creating unreliable narrators

Ask students to write a checklist of ways for writers to create an unreliable narrator – using examples from the Student Book extracts and other books they have read (plus films and TV programmes they have watched).

Extra Time

Ask students to read all of 'The Tell-Tale Heart' and give their reactions to it.

 Weblink   Presentation   ▣ Interactive activity

Lesson focus

Why are we teaching this?

In this lesson, students will explore how poets use figurative language to illustrate essential truths and enable their readers to view the familiar in unexpected ways. Through reading and analysing William Blake's poem 'A Poison Tree' and an extract from T.S. Eliot's 'The Love Song of J. Alfred Prufrock', students will explore and practise writing extended metaphors.

What are students learning?

Students will be able to:

- investigate how and why writers use extended metaphors.

How you could teach this

A variety of activities and approaches are provided on the right for you to select from and adapt to meet the needs of your students. The Kerboodle lesson player sequence is derived from these suggestions, to act as a starting point for your lesson.

Answers

Answers to Student Book activities, where relevant, can be found on page 85.

Teaching suggestions

Ignition

Definitions

Ask students to provide definitions for the following key terms: figurative language, metaphor, personification. Encourage them to provide examples for each one.

Extending a metaphor

Before students read the extract in the Student Book, display the opening line of 'The Love Song of J. Alfred Prufrock': 'The yellow fog that rubs its back upon the window-panes'. Challenge students to extend this metaphor by adding new lines to the poem as they pass it around the class.

Fog

Display the 'Images of fog' image gallery on Kerboodle. Ask students to use figurative language to describe the images being shown. Share some student examples and discuss their effectiveness.

Resources
Kerboodle: 3.3 Images of fog

Exploration

Similes and metaphors

Use the 'Similes and metaphors' interactive activity on Kerboodle to double-check students' understanding of these terms.

Resources
Kerboodle: 3.3 Similes and metaphors

Personal response

Ask students to read the extract from 'The Love Song of J. Alfred Prufrock' on page 64 of the Student Book. Allow them time to discuss their personal responses to the poem with a partner – identifying interesting imagery and discussing its effectiveness – before asking for feedback.

Shared reading

Support Activity 1a in the Student Book by using shared reading of the extract on page 64 to identify the different qualities associated with cats (e.g. 'rubs its back', 'Licked its tongue', 'Slipped by the terrace', 'curled once about the house', etc.) that T. S. Eliot is employing to describe the fog. Encourage students to share their views about the effectiveness of this extended metaphor.

Resources
Student Book 2: Activity 1a, page 64

and guidance

Consolidation

Creating metaphors

Use the 'Creating metaphors' worksheet on Kerboodle to support students with Activity 1b in the Student Book. Encourage them to list the qualities associated with their chosen animal before deciding which type of weather they could best describe.

Resources

Student Book 2: Activity 1b, page 64

Kerboodle: 3.3 Creating metaphors

Model reading

Support Activities 2a and 2b in the Student Book by model reading William Blake's 'A Poison Tree' on page 65. Identify the imagery that Blake uses to create his extended metaphor and comment on what emotional responses the various images might evoke in the reader.

Resources

Student Book 2: Activities 2a and 2b, page 65

'Sonnet 18'

You could challenge higher-achieving students to use the 'Sonnet 18' worksheet on Kerboodle to explore the figurative language being used by Shakespeare in this poem.

Resources

Kerboodle: 3.3 'Sonnet 18' by William Shakespeare

Performing the poem

Ask students to choose one of the poems studied in this lesson to rehearse and perform to the rest of the class.

Evaluation

Ask students to swap the extended metaphors they created in response to Activity 1b with a partner. Encourage them to rate each other's extended metaphors for appropriateness and effectiveness.

Storyboarding the poem

Ask students to create a video to accompany a reading of one of the poems they have studied in this lesson. Emphasize that the video should help to illustrate the extended metaphor being used by the poet. You could use the 'Storyboarding the poem' worksheet on Kerboodle to support this task.

Resources

Kerboodle: 3.3 Storyboarding the poem

The Lamb

Show the class William Blake's poem 'The Lamb' (provided on Kerboodle) and discuss the extended metaphor being used – and its appropriateness.

Resources

Kerboodle: 3.3 'The Lamb' by William Blake

Extra Time

Ask students to find some other poems that include extended metaphors.

🔗 Weblink   🖵 Presentation   🔝 Interactive activity

Lesson focus

Why are we teaching this?

In this lesson, students will use two short extracts from *Alice's Adventures in Wonderland* to explore how wordplay and puns can be used to entertain the reader and create humorous effects. They will also have the opportunity to create their own comic script of a conversation based around puns, wordplay and misunderstandings – inspired by Lewis Carroll's extract, but transplanted to a modern-day setting.

What are students learning?

Students will be able to:

- consider how puns and other forms of wordplay can be used to create humour.

How you could teach this

A variety of activities and approaches are provided on the right for you to select from and adapt to meet the needs of your students. The Kerboodle lesson player sequence is derived from these suggestions, to act as a starting point for your lesson.

> **Answers**
>
> Answers to Student Book activities, where relevant, can be found on page 85.

Teaching suggestions

Ignition

Sounds pun-ful

Display the 'Puns' presentation on Kerboodle, one pun at a time, and ask students to rate each pun, using a 'groanometer' – with the loudest groans given to the very worst puns.

Resources
Kerboodle: 3.4 Puns

Getting punning

Challenge students to suggest their own puns. For example: 'A policeman saw a woman driving a car and knitting at the same time. "Pull over!" he shouted. "No, it's a scarf," she replied.'

Alice in Wonderland

Ask the class what they already know about Lewis Carroll's famous children's story *Alice's Adventures in Wonderland*. Then show the official film trailer for Tim Burton's interpretation of the story (look on YouTube under 'Alice in Wonderland official trailer') and discuss students' impressions of Burton's Wonderland.

Exploration

Model reading

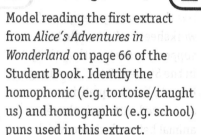

Model reading the first extract from *Alice's Adventures in Wonderland* on page 66 of the Student Book. Identify the homophonic (e.g. tortoise/taught us) and homographic (e.g. school) puns used in this extract.

Wordplay

You could support Activity 1 in the Student Book by asking students to use the 'Wordplay lessons' interactive activity on Kerboodle to match up the puns from the second Student Book extract on page 67 with their real-world subjects.

Resources
Student Book 2: Activity 1, page 66

Kerboodle: 3.4 Wordplay lessons

Dramatic performance

Ask students, working in small groups, to create a dramatic interpretation of the scene described in the second Student Book extract (page 67). Encourage them to consider how they will portray the roles of the different fantastical characters, and also how they could use intonation, tone and volume to emphasize the puns being used for dramatic effect.

and guidance

Consolidation

Alice's Adventures Under Ground

Use the weblink below to display Lewis Carroll's original manuscript for *Alice's Adventures Under Ground* (the original version of *Alice's Adventures in Wonderland*). Discuss the origin of the story, the audience it was written for and how this might have influenced Lewis Carroll's use of puns and wordplay in the story. You could also compare the version of the scene with the Mock Turtle in *Alice's Adventures Under Ground* (pages 80-81 on the weblink version) with the extract in the Student Book and discuss what changes Lewis Carroll made to the text in the final version.

Resources
Weblink: http://www.bl.uk/onlinegallery/ttp/alice/accessible/introduction.html

Vocabulary

Suggest that students use a dictionary to look up key words from the extract on page 67 to help them explore the puns being used. Discuss the rationale behind selected vocabulary choices, e.g. 'reeling and writhing' is a pun on the term 'reading and writing', but could also refer to 'reeling' in a 'writhing' fish and is suggestive of the discomfort of school.

Performing the comic scripts

After students have completed Activity 3 in the Student Book – and finished writing their comic scripts – encourage them to perform them (using intonation, tone, volume, mood, silence, stillness and action to add humour to their improvisations).

Resources
Student Book 2: Activity 3, page 66

Extra Time

Ask students to find and list some puns used in everyday life. For instance, ask them to look at the names of local hairdressing salons. Ask them to explain how the puns they find work.

Evaluation

If you decide to use the 'Performing the comic scripts' Exploration activity, you could follow this up by asking students to rate each other's comic improvisations. Explain that they should use a scale from 1 to 5 for their ratings (with 5 being the highest), and that they should evaluate how effectively each student performer has used puns and wordplay and methods of performance (such as intonation and actions) to create humour.

Pun timetable

Drawing on the puns used in students' own comic scripts, create a class timetable of new school subjects. Ask students to rate the puns created originally and then to suggest further puns inspired by the new subjects.

Podcast

Ask students to create a podcast that discusses the puns and wordplay used in the second Student Book extract from *Alice's Adventures in Wonderland*, and which also presents their personal responses. Encourage them to comment on the effectiveness of the extract's humour for a modern audience.

  Weblink    Presentation   Interactive activity   **75**

Lesson focus

Why are we teaching this?

The theme of the differences between outward appearance and inner reality is an important one in many folk and fairy tales. This lesson will give students the opportunity to explore an extract from the Brothers Grimm folk tale 'Bearskin' and to draw on their knowledge of both the theme and the folk tale form to continue the story in their own writing.

What are students learning?

Students will be able to:

- evaluate the way in which folk tales exploit the theme of outward appearance.

How you could teach this

A variety of activities and approaches are provided on the right for you to select from and adapt to meet the needs of your students. The Kerboodle lesson player sequence is derived from these suggestions, to act as a starting point for your lesson.

> **Answers**
>
> Answers to Student Book activities, where relevant, can be found on page 85.

Teaching suggestions

Ignition

Million-pound challenge

Ask students to vote on whether they would be prepared not to wash or change their clothes for seven years – if it meant that they would then win £1 million for completing the challenge successfully. Discuss the reasons for students' decisions and explore what the possible consequences of not washing or changing your clothes for seven years might be!

Bearskin

Show the class the 'Bearskin' image gallery. Ask students to discuss what they can tell and how they feel about the character depicted in the images. Encourage them to consider whether the character's outward appearance might not necessarily reflect their inner personality.

Resources
Kerboodle: 3.5 Bearskin

Activating prior knowledge

Ask students to make a list of folk and fairy tales they know and then discuss how the themes of identity, deception, appearance and reality are presented in these stories. Take feedback and discuss students' views about why these themes appear so often in folk and fairy tales.

Resources
Student Book 2: Activity 1, page 68

Exploration

Folk and fairy tales

Use the 'Folk and fairy tales' presentation on Kerboodle to discuss the literary and historical context of folk and fairy tales with the class.

Resources
Kerboodle: 3.5 Folk and fairy tales

Checking comprehension

Use the interactive activity on Kerboodle to double-check students' understanding of the events described in the 'Bearskin' extract on pages 70–71 of the Student Book.

Resources
Kerboodle: 3.5 'Bearskin'

Diary entry

Ask students to write a diary entry for the old man's youngest daughter, after she has met Bearskin. Encourage them to empathize with the daughter and to try to express her feelings about the situation she finds herself in. Discuss what different emotions she might feel for Bearskin, her father and her sisters.

and guidance

Exploration

Model reading

Support Activity 2 in the Student Book by model reading the extract from 'Bearskin' to identify textual details that indicate how the soldier has been changed by the experience of becoming Bearskin. Move students from details that demonstrate a literal understanding (e.g. 'long, coarse beard', 'hair matted and tangled'), to the inferences and deductions that can be made from textual details (e.g. the kindness that Bearskin demonstrates to the old man, etc.).

Resources
Student Book 2: Activity 2, page 68

Discussion

Use the 'Statements discussion' worksheet on Kerboodle to prompt students' discussion about the main moral of the 'Bearskin' story. As they consider each statement in turn, encourage them to reflect on the original audience and purpose of the tale, as well as the context in which it was created and passed on.

Resources
Student Book 2: Activity 3, page 69

Kerboodle: 3.5 Statements discussion

Continuing the story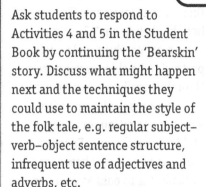

Ask students to respond to Activities 4 and 5 in the Student Book by continuing the 'Bearskin' story. Discuss what might happen next and the techniques they could use to maintain the style of the folk tale, e.g. regular subject–verb–object sentence structure, infrequent use of adjectives and adverbs, etc.

Resources
Student Book 2: Activities 4 and 5, page 69

Ignite English interview

You might like to play Ignite Interview Film 1 to the class. In this film we are introduced to Debbie Korley and her thoughts about acting.

Resources
Kerboodle: 3 Ignite Interview Debbie Korley Film 1

Extra Time

Depending on which Consolidation activity you chose above, you could ask students to read the complete story of 'Bearskin' (and other Grimm's fairy tales that deal with similar themes, such as 'The Frog Prince'). Ask them to compare their own interpretation of the ending of 'Bearskin' with the original version.

Consolidation

Progress Check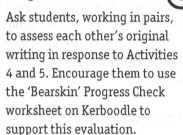

Ask students, working in pairs, to assess each other's original writing in response to Activities 4 and 5. Encourage them to use the 'Bearskin' Progress Check worksheet on Kerboodle to support this evaluation.

Resources
Kerboodle: 3.5 'Bearskin' Progress Check

Comparing endings

Show the class the original ending of the 'Bearskin' folk tale from the weblink below. Discuss any similarities and differences with students' own story endings, and make sure that you allow time for them to share their personal responses to the original version.

Resources
weblink: http://www. scottishstorytellingcentre.co.uk/ festival/TASD12/resources/ Bearskin.pdf

New folk tales

Ask students to brainstorm possible plots for a new folk tale that uses the theme of appearance and reality. Encourage them to think of new ways of presenting this theme using modern settings and characters.

 Weblink   Presentation   Interactive activity   **77**

Lesson focus

Why are we teaching this?

This lesson provides an engaging real-life context for the exploration of the theme of appearance and reality. Students will have the opportunity to read a newspaper article about Frédéric Bourdin (a French conman who took on the identity of a missing Texan schoolboy) and then use it as the impetus for a dramatic exploration of the story.

What are students learning?

Students will be able to:

- explore the ideas and issues around deception and mistaken identity through discussion and improvisation.

How you could teach this

A variety of activities and approaches are provided on the right for you to select from and adapt to meet the needs of your students. The Kerboodle lesson player sequence is derived from these suggestions, to act as a starting point for your lesson.

Answers

Answers to Student Book activities, where relevant, can be found on page 85.

Teaching suggestions

Ignition

Age rating

Display the statement: 'Everybody lies about their age'. Then discuss some reasons why people might pretend to be older or younger than they really are, e.g. to get in to see a particular film with a higher age rating, or to pay a child fare on the bus. Encourage students to consider how easy or difficult it is to pass as younger or older than you really are – referring to anecdotes from their own lives to support their ideas.

The Imposter

Show the class the official trailer for the film *The Imposter* (search on YouTube for 'The Imposter official trailer'). Then share some further details about the real-life Frédéric Bourdin/Nicholas Barclay case. Discuss whether students think it would be possible for an imposter to fool a mother into believing he was her missing son, and how easy it would be.

The perfect disguise

Give students the challenge of fooling a teacher that they are really another student. Ask them to suggest the methods they would use to disguise their real identity and take on another.

Exploration

Discussion

Ask students to discuss Activities 1 and 2 in the Student Book (in small groups or as a whole class). Encourage them to speculate about Frédéric Bourdin's possible motives for pretending to be Nicholas Barclay, as well as possible reasons why the Barclay family chose to accept him as their missing son.

Resources

Student Book 2: Activities 1 and 2, page 72

Discussion strategies

Use the 'Discussion strategies' worksheet on Kerboodle to prompt students' discussions in response to Activities 1 and 2 in the Student Book – encouraging them to use a range of strategies (such as asking questions, empathizing, and relating to their own experience) to interpret the Frédéric Bourdin/ Nicholas Barclay case.

Resources

Student Book 2: Activities 1 and 2, page 72

Kerboodle: 3.6 Discussion strategies

and guidance

Consolidation

Hot-seating

Ask students to work in role as Frédéric Bourdin and members of the Barclay family. Explain that they should take turns to hot-seat each of the characters, with the other students asking questions of each person in role. Ensure that they prepare for the hot-seating by discussing which questions they should ask each person in role. As a starting point, you might want to agree a class list of key questions that need to be answered by the end of the activity. Use the 'Report quotations' presentation on Kerboodle to help with this.

Resources
Kerboodle: 3.6 Report quotations

Improvisation

Before they complete Activity 3 in the Student Book, encourage students (working in small groups) to consider how they could use intonation, tone, volume, mood, silence, stillness and action to add tension and suspense to their improvisations.

Resources
Student Book 2: Activity 3, page 72

Video diary

Follow up Activity 3 in the Student Book by asking students, working in the role of Frédéric Bourdin, to create video diaries in which he shares his thoughts and feelings about his deception. Also encourage them to use the video-diary format to share their speculations about why the Barclay family accepted Bourdin as their missing son – presenting them from Frédéric Bourdin's perspective.

Judge and jury

Ask students to prepare a short summing-up speech from either the prosecution or defence team, to be presented at the end of Frédéric Bourdin's trial. The prosecution speech should explain the impact of Bourdin's actions on the Barclay family, whilst the defence speech should seek to mitigate Bourdin's actions. Use the 'Defence' worksheet on Kerboodle to support students with this aspect of the activity. After the speeches, you could ask the class to vote on the punishment they think Frédéric Bourdin should receive. The real-life Bourdin was sentenced to six years in prison – do students think that was a fair punishment for his deception?

Resources
Kerboodle: 3.6 Defence

Performance

Select groups to perform their improvisations in response to Activity 3 in the Student Book. As a class, identify any dramatic techniques they used to suggest the different characters' thoughts and emotions, and discuss their effectiveness.

Interview

Use the weblink below to play the class a BBC interview with Frédéric Bourdin from 19 October 2012 (when he was 38). Discuss whether this interview changes the impression they have of him, or helps to justify his actions in their eyes. Then ask students to suggest some additional questions that they would like to ask Bourdin.

Resources
Weblink: http://www.bbc.co.uk/news/world-19949847

Progress Check

Two stars and a wish: As an alternative to the peer assessment in the Student Book, you could ask students to pick two things they did well when performing their improvisations and one thing they could improve.

Extra Time

Ask students to carry out more research into the story of Frédéric Bourdin.

Lesson focus

Why are we teaching this?

The themes of appearance and reality, disguise and mistaken identity are often explored in Shakespeare's plays. In this lesson, students will explore an extract from *Twelfth Night* – investigating language use and developing a personal response to the scene through rehearsal and performance.

What are students learning?

Students will be able to:

- develop, through rehearsal and discussion, a personal response to lines from Shakespeare's *Twelfth Night*.

How you could teach this

A variety of activities and approaches are provided on the right for you to select from and adapt to meet the needs of your students. The Kerboodle lesson player sequence is derived from these suggestions, to act as a starting point for your lesson.

Teaching suggestions

Ignition

Film trailer

Show the trailer for the 2012 film adaptation of *Twelfth Night* (search on YouTube for 'Twelfth Night trailer'). Ask some questions to check students' understanding of the premise of the story, before discussing whether this trailer would persuade them to watch the film.

Shakespearean women

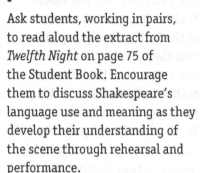

Display the 'Shakespearean women' presentation on Kerboodle. Then encourage students to think about the women in Shakespeare's plays and discuss why they might want or need to pretend to be men. Ask students to make a list of the pros and cons of being a woman in the Elizabethan period (according to this evidence).

Resources
Kerboodle: 3.7 Shakespearean women

Activating prior knowledge

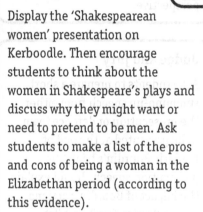

Ask students to suggest any films or TV programmes they have watched, or books they have read, where a character has to impersonate somebody of the opposite gender, e.g. *She's The Man*, *Madame Doubtfire* (the book), *Mrs Doubtfire* (the film), *The Wind in the Willows*, etc. Draw on the suggested examples to discuss how this trope creates humour.

Exploration

Rehearsal and performance

Ask students, working in pairs, to read aloud the extract from *Twelfth Night* on page 75 of the Student Book. Encourage them to discuss Shakespeare's language use and meaning as they develop their understanding of the scene through rehearsal and performance.

Resources
Student Book 2: Activities 1, 2 and 5, page 74

Ignite English interview

You might like to play Ignite Interview Film 1 to the class. In this film we are introduced to Debbie Korley and her thoughts about acting.

Resources
Kerboodle: 3 Ignite Interview Debbie Korley Film 1

Ignite English interview

You might also like to play Ignite Interview Film 2 to the class. In this film Debbie Korley discusses the appeal of Shakespeare and acting.

Resources
Kerboodle: 3 Ignite Interview Debbie Korley Film 2

and guidance

Consolidation

A closer reading

You could support Activities 2–4 in the Student Book by model reading the extract from *Twelfth Night*, in order to demonstrate how to develop an understanding of the events in the scene.

For example, by exploring the connotations of the vocabulary that Duke Orsino uses to describe Cesario's appearance and discussing the dramatic irony of this speech. Alternatively, you could use the 'A closer reading' worksheet on Kerboodle to support students.

Resources

Student Book 2: Activities 2–4, page 74

Kerboodle: A closer reading

Character map

Ask students to create a character map showing the relationships between Duke Orsino, Olivia and Viola/Cesario. Encourage them to discuss what they think will happen in the play and how the themes of disguise and mistaken identity might be developed.

Original pronunciation

Use the weblink below to show the class an interview with Ben and David Crystal about original practices and pronunciation in Shakespearean drama. Discuss students' responses to the examples of original pronunciation shown in the film.

Resources

Weblink: http://worldofwonder. net/shakespeare-in-the-original-pronunciation/

A guide to spying

Ask students to use the weblink below to read a newspaper article about an archived spying handbook for MI5 agents. Then ask them to write an explanation of how to create an effective disguise for a modern guidebook on spying. Encourage them to draw on details from the article when creating their explanation.

Resources

Weblink: http://www.telegraph. co.uk/news/uknews/7393456/ MI5-spying-handbook-ruled-out-use-of-false-beards-and-moustaches.html

Progress Check

Two stars and a wish: Ask students to select two things they did well when performing their scenes and one thing they could improve.

Manga Shakespeare

Ask students to click on and read the series of short articles on the weblink below about the process of creating a graphic-novel version of *Twelfth Night*. Then ask them to create their own graphic-novel retelling of the extract in the Student Book.

Resources

Weblink: http://www. selfmadehero.com/ news/2010/08/nana-li---life-of-a-manga-artist/

Olivia and Viola

Ask students to use the worksheet on Kerboodle to read the scene between Olivia and Viola, before answering the related questions to develop their understanding of the scene.

Resources

Kerboodle: 3.7 Olivia and Viola

Extra Time

Ask students to research the role of women in Shakespeare's theatre.

Lesson focus

Why are we teaching this?

In this lesson students will develop an understanding of the role of the fool in Shakespeare's plays – exploring how the fool's language is used to both entertain and reveal essential truths.

What are students learning?

Students will be able to:

- develop an understanding of the role of the fool in *Twelfth Night*.

How you could teach this

A variety of activities and approaches are provided on the right for you to select from and adapt to meet the needs of your students. The Kerboodle lesson player sequence is derived from these suggestions, to act as a starting point for your lesson.

Teaching suggestions

Ignition

Words from a fool

Display the 'Words from a fool' presentation on Kerboodle. Then ask students to discuss each statement in turn – working out its meaning and suggesting what message it gives about life.

Resources
Kerboodle: 3.8 Words from a fool

Introducing the fool

Display the 'Introducing the fool' presentation on Kerboodle. Check students' understanding of the role of the fool in Shakespeare's plays, as well as in Elizabethan society at large.

Resources
Kerboodle: 3.8 Introducing the fool

Improvisation

Working in pairs, ask students to improvise a scene between two people, where one deliberately misunderstands the other. Encourage them to use intonation, tone, volume, mood, silence, stillness and action to create comic effects in their improvisation.

Exploration

Shared reading

Use shared reading of the dialogue between Olivia and Feste in the extract on page 76 of the Student Book to identify evidence to support Feste's assertion that Olivia is a fool. Discuss whether students agree with Feste.

Resources
Student Book 2: Activity 1, page 77

Looking the fool

Show the 'Looking the fool' image gallery on Kerboodle. Ask students to choose an image to annotate to show the relationship between the characters – drawing on their knowledge of the fool's role.

Resources
Kerboodle: 3.8 Looking the fool

Model reading

Model reading the extract from *Twelfth Night* on page 77 of the Student Book – identifying textual details that demonstrate how Feste is using word play to mock and confuse Viola, e.g. 'I live by the church' misleads Viola into thinking that Feste is a clergyman, when he is actually stating he lives next to a church.

Answers

Answers to Student Book activities, where relevant, can be found on page 85.

and guidance

Rehearsal and performance

Ask students to work in pairs to read aloud the extract on page 77 of the Student Book. Encourage them to discuss the roles of Feste and Viola, and to use intonation, tone and volume to emphasize the word play for comic effect.

A foolish character

Run Activity 4 in the Student Book as a whole-class discussion. Ask students to suggest the different characteristics of a fool that Feste demonstrates in these extracts – providing textual details to support their suggestions. Discuss and agree a class rank order of importance.

Resources
Student Book 2: Activity 4, page 77

21st-century fools

Use the weblink below to present the different types of fool in Shakespeare's plays. Discuss the modern-day equivalents provided in the weblink and ask students to suggest their own modern-day fools from popular culture. Encourage them to justify their choices.

Resources
Weblink: http://www.bbc.co.uk/news/magazine-17476117

Consolidation

Definition of a fool

Ask students to write a definition of the character of 'a fool' for a dictionary about Shakespeare and his plays.

Appraising the fool

Ask students to write in role as Olivia to provide Feste with a work appraisal. As a class, decide on the criteria that Feste's job would be assessed against, e.g. ability to entertain Olivia, speaking the truth, etc. Use the 'Appraising the fool' worksheet on Kerboodle to support this task.

Resources
Kerboodle: 3.8 Appraising the fool

Performing Shakespeare

Agree a class list of top tips for performing Shakespeare.

Extra Time

Ask students to find out more about *Twelfth* Night. For example, they could read a graphic-novel adaptation, watch a film or TV version, or even read the original play!

Assessment focus

Why are we assessing this?

This unit has developed students' critical-reading skills. They have read a range of extracts from fiction, poetry and plays – exploring how the theme of appearance and reality is presented within them, and considering how language (including vocabulary choice, grammar and figurative language) is used to create humour and reveal essential truths. This assessment will enable students to bring these skills together as they write answers to a series of reading questions about an extract from *Madame Doubtfire*.

What are students demonstrating?

Students will be able to comment on how:

- figurative language and vocabulary are used to present meaning
- characterization is developed
- the writer creates humour in the extract.

How to deliver the assessment

Suggestions and guidance on how to set up and prepare your students for the assessment are provided as well as possible approaches to marking the assessment.

Alternative/additional assessment

There is an alternative end-of-unit assessment available on Kerboodle. This assessment leads to a spoken English outcome and can be used either in addition to or instead of the Student Book end-of-unit assessment.

Resources
Kerboodle: 3.9 Alternative end-of-unit assessment

Assessment suggestions and guidance

Understanding the assessment

Check that students understand the assessment task set. Emphasize that they are being tested on their reading skills, and that they should draw on those skills they have developed throughout the unit.

Resources
Student Book 2: pages 78–81

Planning

Remind students that they need to read each question carefully – thinking about exactly what is being asked for and how to present their response.

Completing the assessment

Remind students to refer to evidence and quotations from the text to support their answers.

Timing and writing expectation

Give students one hour (ideally one lesson) and expect approximately one to two A4 pages.

Marking

You will want to mark this in line with departmental and school marking guidelines. If you wish, you could use the Ignite English marking scales provided on Kerboodle. Using the Ignite English marking scales will help you to identify specific strengths and areas for improvement in an individual student's critical reading skills. This may help you to set development targets as well as building a profile of your class as critical readers.

Refer to the KS3 National Curriculum and Ignite English mapping grids on pages 154–156 of this Teacher Companion to identify other Ignite English units where these reading skills are covered, or ask students to use the SPAG interactives on Kerboodle to address any areas identified for improvement. The Grammar Reference Guide on Kerboodle contains definitions and additional examples of each of the spelling, punctuation and grammar points covered in the interactives, for your reference.

Resources
Kerboodle: 3 Ignite English marking scales

Kerboodle: SPAG interactives

Kerboodle: Grammar Reference Guide

Key for Kerboodle LRA resources   📄 Worksheet   🖰 Interactive activity

Student Book answers

Below are the answers to any largely non-subjective Student Book activities contained within this unit.

Lesson 1

1 Students' set designs should show Bailey's chair positioned in the inside row of chairs facing the entrance, with the illusionist initially seated immediately to his left and the chair that appears to catch fire in the section of the circle directly across from Bailey.

Lesson 2

1 Students could comment on how the narrator directly addresses the reader with the question: 'Why will you say that I am mad?' His hearing is described as being impossibly acute, 'I heard all things in the heaven and in the earth', while he attempts to justify his sanity by describing how he planned the old man's murder with great care. Exclamatory sentences such as 'Hearken!' and 'Yes, it was this!' are suggestive of the narrator's agitated state of mind, while the frequent use of dashes reflects the fragmentary nature of the narrator's thought patterns.

3 Students could identify textual details such as Bruno's description of the prisoners as 'pyjama people' indicating that he isn't aware that they are being kept prisoner and the reference to 'sometimes they fell to the ground... didn't even get up' suggesting that he isn't aware that the prisoners are being killed.

Lesson 3

1a Students should identify that Eliot is comparing the fog with a cat, highlighting the qualities associated with cats such as rubbing, muzzling, licking, etc. that are used to describe the fog.

2 Students should identify that Blake is writing about anger in the poem, creating the extended metaphor of cultivating a plant to reflect how he nurtured his own anger.

Lesson 4

1

- reeling and writhing – reading and writing
- ambition, distraction, uglification and derision – addition, subtraction, multiplication and division
- seography – geography
- drawling – drawing
- stretching – sketching
- fainting with coils – painting with oils

Lesson 5

2 Students could comment on:

- Bearskin's physical appearance (i.e. 'long, coarse beard', 'hair matted and tangled', 'Everyone who saw him shuddered or ran away')
- his behaviour and actions (i.e. he initially does whatever he wants, but also makes sure he gives money to the poor to pray for him)
- his thoughts and feelings (i.e. 'how joyfully his heart leaped' when the youngest daughter agrees to marry him).

Lesson 8

1 The reason Feste gives is that Olivia is still mourning her brother, even though she knows that his soul is in Heaven.

2 Students could comment on how Feste is able to question Olivia and refer to her as a fool, even though she is his employer.

3 'A sentence is but a cheveril glove to a good wit' means the meaning of a sentence can be easily changed by a clever mind to cause misunderstanding.

Unit 4: Technology Matters

Unit overview

Why are we teaching this?

Most students are highly skilled users of modern technological devices, and are quick and eager to explore, discuss and (in many cases) acquire innovations. This unit will harness some of this enthusiasm. It will help students to hone and practise their English skills to **explore the impact** of technological innovations, both past and present, and to formulate and **present their own viewpoint** about future technological investment and development.

Students will also examine the importance of English skills in technical texts, by considering how to write specifications for products using precise, clear **instructions**, appropriate **vocabulary** and **grammatical constructions** and a suitable **level of formality**. They will explore how technology can be marketed through the use of a website – focusing, in particular, on **layout and presentational devices**. There are also opportunities to practise **speaking and listening skills** in a group environment, solving technological challenges and justifying their choices.

What are the learning aims?

By the end of the unit, students will be able to:

- use a range of reading strategies, including inference, to explore layers of meaning in a pre-1914 text
- apply their knowledge of grammar, vocabulary and text structure to write in an appropriate form
- read a range of non-fiction texts and draw out relevant information to use in their own writing and presentations
- summarize and organize material to create an effective argument
- speak confidently and effectively in both informal group discussions and formal presentations.

How will this be assessed?

Key assessment task	Focus for assessment
Student Book: Presenting a convincing argument to a government committee to persuade them to back a particular new technology.	- Delivering a carefully structured viewpoint with confidence and clarity. - Speaking in Standard English, using an appropriate level of formality. - Using pace, volume, intonation and eye contact to engage with an audience.
Kerboodle: Writing a formal letter to the school newspaper explaining why money should be spent on a new technology department.	- Expressing a viewpoint with clarity and precision, using Standard English. - Structuring material effectively, supporting ideas and arguments with factual detail. - Using a range of vocabulary, sentence structures and punctuation precisely.

The end-of-unit assessment on Kerboodle can be used either instead of or in addition to the Student Book end-of-unit assessment.

Note that short Progress Checks also feature in this unit, providing formative assessment opportunities to support the students' learning.

Lesson sequence

This is a suggested lesson sequence, but you might choose to alter or add to it to suit your particular teaching needs.

Introducing the unit

1   **Great Innovations**

-   Identify and explain the personal importance of a particular item of technology.
-   Respond to the Ignite Interview featuring Tom Worsley.
-   Discuss major historical technical innovations as a group, agreeing a ranking.
-   Make a sustained contribution to the group discussion, listening and building on what is said.

2 **The Price of Progress**	3 **Selling Technology**	4 **A Clear Message**
<ul><li>Analyse how descriptive devices convey a strong message to the reader.</li><li>Analyse an extract from *Hard Times* by Charles Dickens.</li><li>Write a paragraph inferring Dickens' views about the Industrial Revolution.</li></ul>	<ul><li>Explore how webpages can relay information concisely and promote new products.</li><li>Analyse the effects of a website's presentational devices and layout.</li><li>Summarize the philanthropic activities of Adlens in the developing world.</li></ul>	<ul><li>Write clearly and precisely to convey specific detailed information in Standard English.</li><li>Write a clear product specification, using specific language features.</li><li>Outline a product's key selling points for a sales team to promote.</li></ul>
5 **Disaster!**	6 **Who is Watching You?**	7 **Space Challenge**
<ul><li>Collate and develop material for a short presentation.</li><li>Convey a consistent viewpoint and use an appropriate level of formality.</li><li>Read non-fiction texts about the Gulf Oil Disaster, extracting relevant information.</li><li>Deliver a presentation about the disaster.</li></ul>	<ul><li>Express a point of view clearly in a formal letter to a newspaper.</li><li>Discuss the pros and cons of widespread public surveillance.</li><li>Write a letter to a newspaper's editor, responding to an article about the growing use of spyware by governments.</li></ul>	<ul><li>Participate in a structured group discussion, building on what is said and summarizing the group's conclusions.</li><li>Use logical thought and basic knowledge about science to prioritise items in a survival challenge.</li></ul>

8   **Investing in the Future**

-   Structure a presentation to persuade people to support investment in a particular technology.
-   Show awareness of other arguments that favour alternative options.
-   Weigh up the pros and cons of different energy options.
-   Select a preferred energy option and prepare a presentation to promote it to a government committee.

9   **Assessment**

-   Student Book: Deliver an effective, formal presentation to persuade a government committee to back a particular form of new technology.
-   Kerboodle: Write a formal letter to the school newspaper explaining why money should be spent on a new technology department.

Preparing to teach

Refresh your knowledge

You might find it helpful to refer to the following key points when planning your teaching of this unit.

- Technology shapes our lives today and will continue to do so in the future. Students should be able to intelligently consider and evaluate its impacts, both positive and negative, and be able to use their English skills to read, discuss and form opinions linked to the development of new technologies.

- Innovative technology has played a huge role in the UK economy and will continue to do so – providing jobs at many different levels. The traditional divide between academic subjects and practical/applied subjects has meant that some students feel arts subjects, such as English, will be of little use in their future careers. However, the need to be able to communicate clearly, concisely and at an appropriate level of formality is crucial in most jobs. This unit should engage all students, whatever career path they intend to pursue.

- Technological developments can lead to great power – and the misuse of that power is often a matter of grave debate. Students may wish to consider the development of nuclear and chemical weapons as a less-popular result of technological developments.

- Technological innovations can also raise ethical questions, particularly in the medical field, that students could be encouraged to explore. For example, genetic engineering, fertility treatments and the creation of body organs in laboratory environments are all on-going topics for debate. Emphasize the importance of researching and understanding as many of the facts as possible before deciding on a firm viewpoint.

Links and further reading

- The Science Museum website (http://www.sciencemuseum.org.uk) provides a wealth of stimulating material about science and technology. Look under the 'Educators' section for teaching resources, many of which involve reading, writing and spoken English skills, as well as increasing scientific understanding.

- The World Economic Forum website (http://forumblog.org/2013/04/five-ways-technology-can-help-the-economy/) has interesting features about the benefits of technological innovation in both developed and developing countries.

- The NASA website (http://www.nasa.gov) contains news and features about past, current and future space missions and other aerospace projects.

Much of this material can be adapted for use in reinforcing key English and communication skills.

- *The Gadget Show* website (http://gadgetshow.channel5.com) contains articles, news and videos of the latest innovations – many of which could be used as a stimulus for presentation and discussion skills.

- Students interested in technology may enjoy reading science-fiction novels, which often predict the long-term consequences of technological advances.

Please note that OUP is not responsible for third-party content. Although all links were correct at the time of publication, the content and location of this material may change.

Planning guidance and teaching tips

Think about how you can make the materials relevant to your students and responsive to their needs. Some suggested approaches to address key areas are provided below.

- Encourage students to **read news articles** and magazine features about the latest technological innovations, including: medical advances; the development of green energies and debates about new energy sources; the development of the latest communication and gaming digital devices. Ask students to bring these articles into the lesson, where you could get them to use their **speaking skills to summarize** the article. Any controversial aspects could then be used to provide an up-to-date source for wider class **discussion**.

- In the reading of source texts about technological innovations, ensure that students are aware of the difference between **facts and opinions**. Encourage them to check the sources of information carefully, and to try to assess how **biased** they might be.

- Use the Kerboodle resources to provide appropriate **differentiated** support for students' writing. Skills-based resources link to this unit. Choose those resources that will develop areas of weakness in students' English skills. Ensure an appropriate level of challenge for **gifted and talented** students, e.g. by encouraging more-confident speakers to build arguments for less-popular technological developments, such as nuclear power, GM crops, etc.

- Give students space to talk about and reflect on their independent reading. Creating opportunities for students to discuss and share ideas about a text can help to engage **more-reluctant readers** who have negative attitudes towards reading.

- Many of the activities in this unit are scaffolded using **talk**. Make sure that students are used to working in pairs or small groups, which should be changed regularly to adapt students to working with new people and experiencing different ideas and approaches.

- Refer to the **Grammar Reference Guide** on Kerboodle for definitions and exemplars of the specific grammar and punctuation terms covered in this unit. Kerboodle also provides **SPAG interactives** to help improve the technical accuracy of students' writing and the application of grammar in context. You can assign specific SPAG interactives to individual students or groups of students, according to their needs.

- The **Ignite English interview** films with Tom Worsley provide an insight into the need for good communication skills in engineering. However, you could provide further inspiration and support for students by arranging for an engineer to come into the classroom to talk about recent technological innovations – and to emphasize the use of written and spoken skills in their own workplace.

Lesson focus

Why are we teaching this?

This lesson launches the unit by introducing students to the theme of technological change. It also encourages them to use their speaking and listening skills to explain which item of technology they most value, and also to rank the importance of historical technological innovations – from the wheel to the Internet.

What are students learning?

Students will be able to:

- make a sustained contribution to group discussion, listening and building on what is said.

How you could teach this

A variety of activities and approaches are provided on the right for you to select from and adapt to meet the needs of your students. The Kerboodle lesson player sequence is derived from these suggestions, to act as a starting point for your lesson.

Answers

Answers to Student Book activities, where relevant, can be found on page 107.

Teaching suggestions

Ignition

Ignite English interview

You might like to play Ignite Interview Film 1 to the class. In this film we are introduced to Tom Worsley, engineer, and his thoughts about changing technology. After playing the film, ask students to explain 'process engineering' in their own words. Encourage them to consider the question: 'Is all technology for the greater good?'

Resources
Kerboodle: 4 Ignite Interview Tom Worsley Film 1

Technology you could not live without

Ask students to choose an item of technology that they could not (or at least would not want to) live without. If they need prompting, suggest mobile phone, TV, computer, car, bike. (It doesn't have to be digital.)

Resources
Student Book 2: Activity 1, page 83

Definition

Write 'Technology' on the board and give students, working in pairs, two minutes to write a definition of the term. Take feedback and then display the 'Technology definitions' presentation on Kerboodle. Discuss which definition students prefer and why.

Resources
Kerboodle: 4.1 Technology definitions

Exploration

Understanding innovations

Before students complete Activity 1a in the Student Book, draw their attention to the nine innovations presented in the timeline diagram. Check their understanding about these inventions and invite them to offer any knowledge of their own about each one. If necessary, use the 'Innovations fact sheet' on Kerboodle to provide additional facts about each innovation to enable the groups to discuss its importance.

Resources
Student Book 2: Activity 1a, page 84

Kerboodle: 4.1 Innovations fact sheet

Discussion

If a group's discussion risks being dominated by a few more-confident students, introduce a 'talk stone' (or similar object), which somebody has to be holding before they can speak. Explain that nobody is allowed to interrupt the speaker unless they are passed the 'stone'. This is a good way to ensure that less-confident students are not talked over.

Resources
Student Book 2: Activity 1a, page 84

and guidance

Consolidation

Ranking task

Compare the results of each group's ranking list in response to Activity 1b in the Student Book. You could decide to collate the group rankings to compile an overall class ranking. Encourage discussion between the groups about any different decisions they may have made and their reasons for them.

Resources
Student Book 2: Activity 1b, page 84

Top 10 Inventions of All Time

Ask every group's spokesperson to describe and explain their group's proposed additional tenth item to go on the Student Book list/ diagram. Invite the class to vote on their favourite addition.

Resources
Student Book 2: Activity 1c, page 84

Looking into the future

Refer back to Tom Worsley's idea, in his Ignite English interview, of inventing a time machine. Ask students what they would like to invent and how it might change people's lives.

Resources
Kerboodle: 4 Ignite Interview Tom Worsley Film 1

Extra Time

Ask students to interview an elderly friend or relative to find out which technological changes they think have been the most important so far in their lifetime. Encourage students to ask their interviewees whether they think these changes have been wholly beneficial, or whether they have also brought some disadvantages.

Progress Check

Once students have rated their own speaking and listening skills, in response to the Progress Check in the Student Book, encourage them to share their ratings with a partner and discuss whether they agree or not. Point out that our own perception of our skills may not always be the same as the perceptions of other people.

Resources
Student Book 2: Progress Check, page 85

Summarizing technology

Ask students to create a 140-character tweet to describe their favourite item of digital technology and why they like it so much.

Benefits of technology

Refer back to Tom Worsley's Ignite English interview and ask students whether they agree with his opinion that 'good design will save the world'.

Resources
Kerboodle: 4 Ignite Interview Tom Worsley Film 1

Lesson focus

Why are we teaching this?

This lesson gives students an insight into how the impact of technological change has been viewed historically, as revealed through a literary description from the time. It also gives them the opportunity to use their inference skills to work out the author's (Dickens') personal viewpoint.

What are students learning?

Students will be able to:

- understand how description uses vocabulary, figurative language and text structure to convey a strong message to the reader.

How you could teach this

A variety of activities and approaches are provided on the right for you to select from and adapt to meet the needs of your students. The Kerboodle lesson player sequence is derived from these suggestions, to act as a starting point for your lesson.

Answers

Answers to Student Book activities, where relevant, can be found on page 107.

Teaching suggestions

Ignition

Industrial Revolution

Write 'Industrial Revolution' on the board and give students, working in pairs, three minutes to write a definition of the term, which they may well have come across in their History lessons. Take feedback and use 'The Industrial Revolution' presentation on Kerboodle to ensure that students understand the context of Dickens' novel *Hard Times* before they go on to read the extract in the Student Book.

Resources
Kerboodle: 4.2 The Industrial Revolution

Charles Dickens

Ask students to share their prior knowledge of Charles Dickens. Then show the 'Charles Dickens fact file' presentation on Kerboodle. Explain that Dickens' novels often highlighted the plight of the poor and drew attention to the social changes taking place in Victorian England.

Resources
Kerboodle: 4.2 Charles Dickens fact file

Interpreting an image

Use the weblink below to display the painting 'Pit Tragedy' by L. S. Lowry. Ask students to comment on the depiction of the industrial setting, as well as to speculate on what might have happened.

Resources
Weblink: http://www.bbc.co.uk/arts/yourpaintings/paintings/pit-tragedy-162391

Exploration

Depicting Coketown

Encourage students to respond to Activity 1 in the Student Book by visualizing the fictional town of Coketown, as described by Dickens – in particular, his references to colour. Draw contrasts with the blues, yellows and greens usually depicted in rural scenes.

Resources
Student Book 2: Activity 1, page 86

Vocabulary builder

Encourage students to use a range of strategies to work out the meaning of any new or unfamiliar vocabulary in the Student Book extract, e.g. reading on and looking back to find contextual clues for words such as 'piston' and 'melancholy'.

---

and guidance

Consolidation

Similes and metaphors

Before they tackle Activity 2 in the Student Book, ensure that students' understanding of similes and metaphors is secure, by inviting them to suggest examples of their own.

Resources
Student Book 2: Activity 2, page 86

Industrial sounds

Depending on the location and situation of the classroom, Activity 3 in the Student Book could be extended by asking groups of students to recreate the sounds of a factory. For example, they could use percussion instruments, or stamping, clapping, hissing, banging. Or it could be done using technology – layering sounds to build up a crescendo of noise. You could use a video clip of 'Stomp' performing for inspiration.

Resources
Student Book 2: Activity 3, page 87

Ignite English interview

You might like to play Ignite Interview Film 1 to the class. In this film we are introduced to Tom Worsley and his thoughts about changing technology.

Resources
Kerboodle: 4 Ignite Interview Tom Worsley Film 1

Using inference

Before students complete Activity 5 in the Student Book, encourage some discussion to clarify their ideas. Ask students to look for connotations in the language that Dickens uses, which reveal his feelings.

Resources
Student Book 2: Activity 5, page 87

Alternative description

Use the extract from *The Road to Wigan Pier* on Kerboodle to provide students with George Orwell's description of industrial Wigan in the 1930s. Ask students how Orwell conveys a negative perception of the town in his description.

Resources
Kerboodle: 4.2 An extract from *The Road to Wigan Pier*

Extra Time

Ask students to write a paragraph describing a fictional town in the future. Remind them to convey a clear notion of whether the technological changes described have improved or worsened the town.

Performance

Follow up the 'Industrial sounds' Exploration activity by selecting different student groups to give individual performances of factory/industrial sounds. Comment on whether they create a positive or negative effect with their rhythms and volume. Ask students whether they think they could work in an environment that was constantly full of loud industrial noise.

Reading paragraphs

Follow up Activity 5 in the Student Book by inviting students to read out their paragraphs inferring what Dickens felt about the effects of the Industrial Revolution. Ask the audience to comment on how well they think each student used evidence from the *Hard Times* extract to back up their views.

Figurative language

Ask each student to write one simile and one metaphor to describe something where they live. Take feedback and highlight the most unusual and evocative comparisons.

Lesson focus

Why are we teaching this?

Marketing is an increasingly important part of any business, especially for companies producing innovative new products. English skills play an essential part in writing persuasive promotional materials; employing presentational devices effectively; and creating a powerful and arresting online presence. In this lesson, students explore how one technology company promotes itself and its philanthropic philosophy effectively online.

What are students learning?

Students will be able to:

- explore how webpages can relay information concisely and promote new products.

How you could teach this

A variety of activities and approaches are provided on the right for you to select from and adapt to meet the needs of your students. The Kerboodle lesson player sequence is derived from these suggestions, to act as a starting point for your lesson.

Answers

Answers to Student Book activities, where relevant, can be found on page 107.

Teaching suggestions

Ignition

Selling technology

Ask students to imagine that they have an innovative product to sell. Give them one minute to write a list of features that they want to include on their website to promote their product. If they need a starting point, suggest a product name, slogan, menu, images, etc.

Marketing tips for Tom's sales team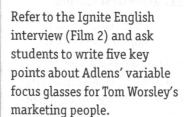

Refer to the Ignite English interview (Film 2) and ask students to write five key points about Adlens' variable focus glasses for Tom Worsley's marketing people.

Resources
Kerboodle: 4 Ignite Interview Tom Worsley Film 2

Favourite website for selling products

Ask students what they buy online and encourage some discussion about the websites they use. Focus on what attracts them to some websites and not to others. Query whether they have ever tried to buy something online and been frustrated by a website that isn't easy to navigate.

Exploration

Using icons

Use the weblink below to show the class the John Lennon section of the Adlens website. Share any knowledge that students may already have about John Lennon – adding relevant information about his style, beliefs and philosophy where necessary. Encourage students to discuss why they think John Lennon is being used to promote Adlens glasses.

Resources
Student Book 2: Activity 1 and Support activity, page 88

Weblink: www.adlens.com/products/john-lennon-collection/

Presentational devices

Encourage students to respond to Activity 2 in the Student Book by identifying all of the relevant presentational devices on the John Lennon webpage and explaining their effects on the reader/viewer. You could extend this activity by looking at other pages on the Adlens weblink below.

Resources
Student Book 2: Activity 2, page 89

Weblink: www.adlens.com

and guidance

Consolidation

Double meanings

Support Activity 3 in the Student Book by ensuring that students understand that 'vision' is used both literally and metaphorically on these webpages.

Resources
Student Book 2: Activity 3, page 89

Quotations and statistics

Support Activities 4 and 5 in the Student Book by drawing out the value of keeping quotations short and statistics to a minimum in promotional/marketing materials. Point out that too much of either will lessen their impact.

Resources
Student Book 2: Activities 4 and 5, page 89

Writing a summary

Before students complete Activity 6 in the Student Book, display the 'Rules for writing a summary' presentation on Kerboodle. Go through the rules and examples to ensure that students have a firm grasp of summarizing techniques.

Resources
Student Book 2: Activity 6, page 89

Kerboodle: 4.3 Rules for writing a summary

Medical technology

Ask students to think of other ways in which technological developments have given people a better quality of life – and even extended or saved lives. Draw out medical examples such as mobility, prosthetic limbs, hearing aids, diagnosis using scans, laser treatments and chemotherapy, etc.

Extra Time

Ask students to research another website that promotes a technological product and to analyse how it uses layout and presentational devices to create particular effects on the reader. They should be prepared to discuss their findings in pairs or small groups.

Sharing summaries

Ask students to swap their summaries from Activity 6 with a partner. Explain that each student has to try to identify ways in which their partner's text could be more concise – deleting unnecessary words and rephrasing sentences. Share some final summaries with the whole class.

Celebrity endorsement

Challenge students to think of five celebrities who endorse different products. This could be a timed challenge for pairs. They then have to explain why they think each celebrity was chosen by the advertiser to promote that particular product. The winning pair will be the first one with five well-explained answers.

Briefing a web designer

Ask students to create a checklist of key features that they would include in a brief to a webpage designer for a new product. If they made a list at the start of the lesson, students could compare both lists and see what additional ideas they have developed.

 Weblink   Presentation   Interactive activity

Lesson focus

Why are we teaching this?

The ability to communicate fluently and in detail, both in spoken English and in writing, is an important skill in many jobs. Even students who are more enthusiastic about Science, Maths, Engineering and practical skills – rather than English – will benefit from honing their spoken and written English skills. This unit gives a very practical demonstration of the importance of these skills.

What are students learning?

Students will be able to:

- write clearly and precisely to convey specific detailed information in Standard English.

How you could teach this

A variety of activities and approaches are provided on the right for you to select from and adapt to meet the needs of your students. The Kerboodle lesson player sequence is derived from these suggestions, to act as a starting point for your lesson.

Answers

Answers to Student Book activities, where relevant, can be found on page 107.

Teaching suggestions

Ignition

Ignite English Interview

Watch the interview clip where Tom Worsley explains what a product specification is (Film 2). Then discuss a manufacturer's need for precision.

Resources

Kerboodle: 4 Ignite Interview Tom Worsley Film 2

Technical descriptions

Give a brief technical description of a knife and ask students to guess what you are describing. Give out details one at a time. For example: 'It has a serrated edge; it is made of stainless steel; it is 16 cm long', etc.

Draw it!

Ask students, working in pairs, to describe the physical appearance of a manufactured product, while their partner uses the verbal description to draw it. (Emphasize that they are not allowed to name the product in their description, or say what it's used for.) As soon as the 'drawer' guesses the product correctly, the roles are reversed. The pair that correctly identifies the most items in the allotted time wins.

Exploration

A new product

Support Activity 1 in the Student Book by asking students to come up with an idea for a new product that would appeal to a teenage market. After reminding them of Tom Worsley's comments about drawing his ideas, encourage students to sketch and annotate their product. Emphasize that this activity is about the use of English, rather than needing to explore in great detail the technological workings of the product.

Resources

Student Book 2: Activity 1, page 92

iPhone case specification

Before students attempt Activity 2 in the Student Book, go through the model product specification for an iPhone case on page 93 of the Student Book and ensure that students understand the language features being referred to.

Resources

Student Book 2: Activity 2, page 92

and guidance

Consolidation

An existing product

A less-challenging approach towards Activities 1 and 2 in the Student Book would be to give students a choice of existing items (e.g. a shoe, a pen, a piece of sports equipment) and ask them to draw up what they think could have been in the original product specification.

Resources

Student Book 2: Activities 1 and 2, page 92

Grammar practice

You could support Activity 2 in the Student Book by using the Grammar Reference Guide SPAG interactives on Kerboodle to consolidate students' knowledge about subordinate clauses, the passive voice and modal verbs.

Resources

Student Book 2: Activity 2, page 92

Kerboodle: Grammar Reference Guide SPAG interactives

Product specification

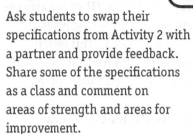

If desired, you could provide the 'Product specification template' on Kerboodle for students to write into for Activity 2.

Resources

Student Book 2: Activity 2, page 92

Kerboodle: 4.4 Product specification template

Marketing messages

Before they respond to Activity 3 in the Student Book, encourage students to think carefully about which aspects of their particular product would appeal the most to their target market (teenagers). Emphasize that they should also consider which choice of vocabulary would appeal to the target market, and decide a pricing policy. This could be extended into drafting a whole advertising campaign.

Resources

Student Book 2: Activity 3, page 92

Extra Time

Ask students to choose a domestic item and write a technical, physical description of it – using clear precise detail and without naming the item. They should then read their description to a partner, who must guess the name of the item.

Progress Check

Ask students to swap their specifications from Activity 2 with a partner and provide feedback. Share some of the specifications as a class and comment on areas of strength and areas for improvement.

Resources

Student Book 2: Progress Check, page 93

Grammar check

Ask students to work in pairs and complete the 'Grammar' interactive activity on Kerboodle.

Resources

Kerboodle: 4.4 Grammar

Identifying key features

Display the 'Production specification' interactive activity on Kerboodle and challenge particular students to come up to the front and decide whether the statement you are indicating is true or false, before dragging it to the correct column.

Resources

Kerboodle: 4.4 Production specification

Lesson focus

Why are we teaching this?

Sifting through information to find key points is a valuable skill, which this lesson gives students the opportunity to practise – with the purpose of gathering relevant material for a short presentation. (They can also use additional resources to supplement their presentations.) This lesson considers the downside of technology – when it goes spectacularly wrong.

What are students learning?

Students will be able to:

- collate and develop material for a short presentation
- convey a consistent viewpoint and use an appropriate level of formality.

How you could teach this

A variety of activities and approaches are provided on the right for you to select from and adapt to meet the needs of your students. The Kerboodle lesson player sequence is derived from these suggestions, to act as a starting point for your lesson.

Answers

Answers to Student Book activities, where relevant, can be found on page 107.

Teaching suggestions

Ignition

Famous disasters

Write 'Chernobyl', '*Challenger* space shuttle' and 'Gulf oil spill' on the board. Ask students what they know about these events and what they have in common. Draw out that they were all failures of technology. Use the 'Background to the disasters' presentation on Kerboodle to provide additional background information about these three disasters.

Resources

Kerboodle: 4.5 Background to the disasters

Disaster images

Show the class the 'Disaster!' image gallery on Kerboodle. Encourage students to speculate about what each image shows (the sinking of the *Titanic*; the *Challenger* shuttle explosion; the Gulf oil spill) and how it links up with technology or technological failure. You could also use the weblink below to show a short video of the *Challenger* shuttle disaster.

Resources

Kerboodle: 4.5 Disaster!

Weblink: www.bbc.co.uk/news/magazine-12306318

When technology goes wrong

Ask students if they can think of a time when technology has gone wrong. Start with domestic struggles with computers and TVs. Scale out to oil spills, nuclear reactors leaking, plane crashes, etc.

Exploration

Additional resources

You might like to offer students some additional resources for their research on the Gulf oil spill. The 'Gulf oil spill additional resources' worksheet on Kerboodle provides two further articles for students to read.

Resources

Student Book 2: Activity 1, page 94

Kerboodle: 4.5 Gulf oil spill additional resources

Images for the presentation

If students wish to include visuals in their presentations, as part of Step 3, you could suggest that they key 'free images of Gulf oil spill' into an Internet search engine.

Resources

Student Book 2: Activity 2, page 95

Planning the presentation

You could use the 'Presentation planning template' worksheet on Kerboodle to support those students who need further help in structuring their presentations.

Resources

Student Book 2: Activity 2, page 95

Kerboodle: 4.5 Presentation planning template

Key for Kerboodle LRA resources Lesson Player Image Video Worksheet

and guidance

Rehearsing the presentation

Encourage students to work in pairs to rehearse their presentations – making suggestions to each other about how they could improve both the content and the delivery.

Resources
Student Book 2: Activity 3, page 95

How to present

Ask students to work in pairs to produce a five-point advice poster about presenting. Encourage them to focus on aspects such as voice, eye contact, body language, pace and intonation. Display the best posters.

Presentation notes

Some students might benefit from having brief reminder notes written out in front of them, rather than their whole presentation. Encourage these students to write notes summarizing their material – using techniques such as key words, bullet points, highlights and headings.

Consolidation

Presenting to a group

Group students and ask them to present their work to each other. Say that the audience should comment on two aspects of the presentation that are strong and one area that could be improved.

Presenting to the class

Invite one or two students to give their presentations to the class as a whole. Explain that the audience should feed back comments, with reference to the five-point advice poster created in the 'How to present' Exploration activity.

Effect of technology disasters

Refer back to the Big Question at the start of the unit: 'Do technological advances always benefit us?' Ask students if their work this lesson has influenced their initial responses to the Big Question and why or why not.

Extra Time

Ask students to do some research of their own to find out more information to include in their presentation about the Gulf oil spill. In particular, suggest that they look at the longer-term effects of the spill.

Lesson focus

Why are we teaching this?

Students are often keen to express their views and opinions in an informal way – usually orally – but are less accustomed to writing them down in a formal letter that might be suitable for publication or wider public discussion. This lesson offers students the opportunity to practise expressing their viewpoint formally, by writing a letter to a newspaper editor. The content focus is on the increasing use of technology by governments for surveillance – an important and controversial topic.

What are students learning?

Students will be able to:

- express a point of view clearly in a formal letter to a newspaper.

How you could teach this

A variety of activities and approaches are provided on the right for you to select from and adapt to meet the needs of your students. The Kerboodle lesson player sequence is derived from these suggestions, to act as a starting point for your lesson.

Answers

Answers to Student Book activities, where relevant, can be found on page 107.

Teaching suggestions

Ignition

Who is Big Brother?

Write 'Big Brother' on the board and ask students what they understand by this term. If necessary, explain its origins in George Orwell's novel *1984*, and its subsequent use in everyday language (including its use as the title of the reality TV show).

Surveillance too far

Display the following announcement on the board and ask students to discuss it: 'Some students have been writing graffiti on the walls of the toilets. The school governors have now decided to install security cameras in all toilets to prevent it happening again.'

If I were a spy …

Ask students what secret technological devices (excluding weapons) they would want to have if they were spies. Encourage speculation about fictional/futuristic devices and how they could be concealed as well as used.

Exploration

Summarizing views

Encourage students to respond initially to Activity 1 in the Student Book by discussing the pros and cons of surveillance with a partner. Then they have to summarize their own personal viewpoint about the issue in a tweet of 140 characters or less.

Resources
Student Book 2: Activity 1, page 98

Context

Before Students complete Activity 2a in the Student Book, discuss as a class how increasing amounts of personal data are being gathered and stored whenever people use the Internet or mobile phones. Ensure that students are aware of the wider picture before reading the Student Book article.

Resources
Student Book 2: Activity 2a, page 98

Big Brother Watch

Either ask students what they already know about the organization Big Brother Watch, or ask them to speculate about what it might be. Then use the weblink below to show the organization's website – pointing out their slogan: 'defending civil liberties, protecting privacy'.

Resources
Weblink: www.bigbrotherwatch.org.uk

and guidance

Consolidation

Monologue

Ask students to write a brief monologue entitled 'A day in the life of a CCTV camera'. Encourage them to convey their opinion about the value of CCTV cameras through their monologue.

Letter to the editor

Use the 'Letter to the editor' worksheet on Kerboodle to support students when they complete Activity 2b in the Student Book.

Resources

Student Book 2: Activity 2b, page 98

Kerboodle: 4.6 Letter to the editor

Standard English

If appropriate, revise students' understanding of Standard English. Ask students to work in pairs to write two sentences, both about surveillance, with one in Standard English and the other in non-Standard English. Draw out that the use of slang, colloquialisms, question tags, abbreviations, etc. are all considered non-Standard English.

Resources

Student Book 2: Activity 2b, page 98

Alternative stimulus article

As an alternative to the article on page 99 of the Student Book, you could instead ask students to respond formally to the editor of the article on Kerboodle about the controversial use of the Mosquito device to deter young people from gathering in public places. Or you could split the class and ask half of the students to respond to each article.

Resources

Kerboodle: 4.6 Alternative 'Mosquito' article

Extra Time

Ask students to find an example of a well-crafted letter to a newspaper editor (not just online comments in response to an online newspaper article). They should bring in a print copy and be prepared to explain why they think it's a well-written letter.

Reading monologues

If you used the 'Monologue' Exploration activity, invite several students to read out their monologues. Ask the audience whether they think the writers are for or against such surveillance, and why.

Formal letters

Share some of the formal letters to the newspaper editor with the class. Invite comments about the content and the suitability of the writing style for this format.

Spot the mistakes

Use the 'High Speed Rail Link' presentation on Kerboodle to display the informal made-up letter to the editor. Ask students to identify any use of language, vocabulary and phrasing that would be considered inappropriate in a formal letter. Then display the real version, which was published in the *Daily Telegraph*.

Resources

Kerboodle: 4.6 High Speed Rail Link

 Weblink   Presentation   Interactive activity

Lesson focus

Why are we teaching this?

The dynamics of group discussion are often complex, so this lesson gives students guidance and practice in their listening, speaking and thinking skills. It also gives real-life examples that show the importance of being able to work productively as a group – in particular during space exploration.

What are students learning?

Students will be able to:

- participate in a structured group discussion, building on what is said and summarizing the group's conclusions.

How you could teach this

A variety of activities and approaches are provided on the right for you to select from and adapt to meet the needs of your students. The Kerboodle lesson player sequence is derived from these suggestions, to act as a starting point for your lesson.

Answers

Answers to Student Book activities, where relevant, can be found on page 107.

Teaching suggestions

Ignition

Apollo 13 crisis

Ask students what they already know about the Apollo 13 mission to the Moon, which was dramatised in the film featuring Tom Hanks. Give some background information about the mission and then use the weblink below to play some of the video clip. Emphasize that the three astronauts survived by using their initiative, and the initiative of colleagues at NASA, to adapt a very limited amount of equipment to a role it wasn't originally designed for.

Resources
Weblink: www.bbc.co.uk/science/space/solarsystem/space_missions/apollo_13#p009xqpv 🔗

Space capsule

Challenge students to choose just ten items to be placed in a space capsule being sent into outer space by NASA – with the aim of conveying information about the human race to any alien life form that might come across it. They should work in pairs or small groups before feeding back.

Astronaut interview

Use the weblink below to play students part of a TV interview conducted by Jeremy Paxman with Major Tim Peake (the first British astronaut selected to visit the International Space Station in 2015). In particular, focus on why Major Peake was selected – drawing out his ability to cooperate with people.

Resources
Weblink: www.bbc.co.uk/news/science-environment-22612053 🔗

Exploration

Pros and cons

Ask students to begin this activity by reading the newspaper review article on Kerboodle about the TV interview between Major Tim Peake and Jeremy Paxman on *Newsnight*. Then, depending on their point of view, ask students (working in pairs) to write a list of five reasons either in favour of or against sending a British astronaut into space.

Resources
Kerboodle: 4.7 Peake/Paxman interview article 📄

NASA background

Activate students' prior knowledge about NASA, including its history and role in developing cutting-edge technology. Refer to the 'NASA fact file' on Kerboodle and/or the NASA website below for up-to-date information about space projects and other new technologies.

Resources
Kerboodle: 4.7 NASA fact file 🖥

Weblink: www.nasa.gov 🔗

and guidance

Consolidation

Moon facts

As a class, read the 'Moon facts' panel on page 101 of the Student Book before students attempt the group challenge in Activity 1. Ensure that students understand these basic facts about the Moon, because they will need to use them when completing their survival challenge.

Resources
Student Book 2: Activity 1, page 100

Survival challenge

Remind students that Activity 1 in the Student Book is a test of their discussion skills, as well as a problem-solving challenge. Walk around the different groups as they discuss the Student Book problem, noting examples of good communication and co-operation.

Resources
Student Book 2: Activity 1, page 100

Note taking

If required, use the 'Note-taking skills' presentation on Kerboodle to remind students about the key skills of note taking.

Resources
Student Book 2: Activity 1, page 100

Kerboodle: 4.7 Note-taking skills

Ignite English interview

You might like to play Ignite Interview Film 2 to the class, in which Tom Worsley discusses communication skills.

Resources
Kerboodle: 4 Ignite Interview Tom Worsley Film 2

Reporting back

Invite some students to report back on their group's ranking of the 15 items of equipment. Encourage them to explain the reasons behind their ranking. Then display the ranking recommended by two NASA experts, as outlined on their website.

Resources
Student Book 2: Activity 1, page 100

Weblink: www.nasa.gov (search using key words 'Survival challenge' and download the pdf. Scroll down to pages 26–9 for the rankings)

Progress Check

If students completed a similar Progress Check in Lesson 1, encourage them to compare their results with this one to see if and how they have progressed in their speaking and listening skills.

Teacher commentary

Share with students some of the examples of good communication and co-operation that you observed during the group discussions. Emphasize that it's not always the person who speaks the most and the loudest in a group discussion who necessarily contributes the most useful thoughts.

Extra Time

Ask students to write the mission's log entries before and after their journey to the outpost.

 Weblink   Presentation   Interactive activity

Lesson focus

Why are we teaching this?

The development and application of new technologies opens up many options for society. Evaluating those options, forming opinions and presenting a viewpoint are important skills – not just for English. This lesson gives students the opportunity to practise those skills, by focusing on the issue of future energy supplies. It also provides the groundwork and preparation for the end-of-unit assessment presentation next lesson.

What are students learning?

Students will be able to:

- structure a presentation to persuade people to support investment in a particular technology
- show awareness of other arguments that favour alternative options.

How you could teach this

A variety of activities and approaches are provided on the right for you to select from and adapt to meet the needs of your students. The Kerboodle lesson player sequence is derived from these suggestions, to act as a starting point for your lesson.

Answers

Answers to Student Book activities, where relevant, can be found on page 107.

Teaching suggestions

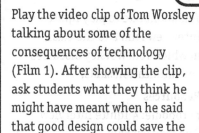

Ignition

Who needs energy?

Ask students to list all the times that they have used generated energy to do something today (i.e. used an energy source other than their own body). The list might start: 'woke up to radio alarm; checked messages on mobile; switched on light, etc. Ask them to imagine their life without energy sources.

Ignite English Interview

Play the video clip of Tom Worsley talking about some of the consequences of technology (Film 1). After showing the clip, ask students what they think he might have meant when he said that good design could save the world in the end.

Resources
Kerboodle: 4 Ignite Interview Tom Worsley Film 1

An Inconvenient Truth

Use the weblink below to show the class the trailer for Al Gore's film documentary *An Inconvenient Truth*. Discuss what message he is trying to deliver about the future of the planet. Draw out that global warming, largely caused by humans burning fossil fuels and depleting the ozone layer, has the potential to cause disastrous long-term consequences.

Resources
Weblink: http://www.imdb.com/video/screenplay/vi2897608985/ 🔗

Exploration

Choosing an option

Encourage students to discuss the information about the three main energy options on pages 103–105 of the Student Book before making their choice about which option to promote in their end-of-unit presentation. Higher-attaining students might enjoy the challenge of promoting nuclear energy. Fracking for shale gas is just one choice in relation to fossil fuels. Others might include coal mining or drilling for oil.

Resources
Student Book 2: Activity 1, page 102

Researching the presentation

You could use the 'Energy debate: extra resources' worksheet on Kerboodle to offer students additional articles to inform their presentations. If necessary, remind them how to make efficient notes – using key words and phrases; noting source details; including quotations. Encourage students to rephrase important points in their own words, rather than just cutting and pasting large sections of text from elsewhere.

Resources
Student Book 2: Activity 2, page 102

Kerboodle: 4.8 Energy debate: extra resources

and guidance

Consolidation

Structuring your presentation

Distribute the 'Presentation planning template' on Kerboodle to help students to structure their presentations.

Resources

Student Book 2: Activities 3 and 4, page 102

Kerboodle: 4.8 Presentation planning template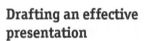

Drafting an effective presentation

Ask students, working in pairs, to compile a checklist for drafting (not delivering) an effective presentation. Take feedback and compile a class list. The checklist presentation on Kerboodle might be helpful, but encourage students to think for themselves before displaying the presentation and adding to it.

Resources

Student Book 2: Activity 4, page 102

Kerboodle: 4.8 Drafting an effective presentation: checklist

Counter-argument

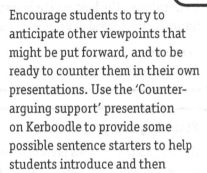

Encourage students to try to anticipate other viewpoints that might be put forward, and to be ready to counter them in their own presentations. Use the 'Counter-arguing support' presentation on Kerboodle to provide some possible sentence starters to help students introduce and then counter other viewpoints.

Resources

Student Book 2: Activity 5, page 102

Kerboodle: 4.8 Counter-arguing support

Peer assessment

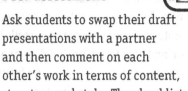

Ask students to swap their draft presentations with a partner and then comment on each other's work in terms of content, structure and style. The checklist on Kerboodle could be referred to if necessary.

Resources

Kerboodle: 4.8 Drafting an effective presentation: checklist

Self-evaluation

Two stars and a wish: ask students to decide on two things they did well in their presentation planning and one thing they could improve.

Extra Time

Ask students to do some additional research to improve their presentation before they present it next lesson. This might involve finding suitable images, quotations or statistics to reinforce their viewpoint.

Assessment focus

Why are we assessing this?

Students have completed a unit focusing on the theme of technology – using their reading, writing and spoken English skills to explore issues related to technological change and its impacts. This assessment tests how well students can use some of those skills by requiring them to create and deliver a persuasive presentation to guide future investment in energy technology.

What are students demonstrating?

Students will be able to:

- deliver a formal presentation, giving a viewpoint and showing awareness of counter-arguments.

How to deliver the assessment

Suggestions and guidance on how to set up and prepare your students for the assessment are provided as well as possible approaches to marking the assessment.

Alternative/additional assessment

There is an alternative end-of-unit assessment available on Kerboodle. This assessment leads to a written outcome and can be used either in addition to or instead of the Student Book end-of-unit assessment.

Resources
Kerboodle: 4.9 Alternative
end-of-unit assessment

Assessment suggestions and guidance

Understanding the assessment

Check that students understand the assessment task set. Emphasize that they are being tested on their *spoken* English skills, and that they should draw on the preparatory work completed in the previous lesson. This task has been set as a formal presentation to a government committee, which is considering the best way to invest public money to guide research into future technological developments in the energy field.

Resources
Student Book 2: pages 106–107

Planning and preparation

The preparation for this presentation should already have been completed in the previous lesson and for homework. Remind students that they should include their plans as part of their assessment.

Completing the assessment

Remind students to rehearse their presentation – alone. Students must complete the assessment individually, so that an accurate mark or level can be given.

Marking

You will want to mark this in line with departmental and school marking guidelines. If you wish, you could use the Ignite English marking scales provided on Kerboodle. Using the Ignite English marking scales will help you to identify specific strengths and areas for improvement in an individual student's spoken English skills. This may help you to set development targets as well as build a profile of your class as speakers.

Refer to the KS3 National Curriculum and Ignite English mapping grids on pages 154–156 of this Teacher Companion to identify other Ignite English units where these spoken English skills are covered, or ask students to use the SPAG interactives on Kerboodle to address any areas identified for improvement. The Grammar Reference Guide on Kerboodle contains definitions and additional examples of each of the spelling, punctuation and grammar points covered in the interactives, for your reference.

Resources
Kerboodle: 4 Ignite English marking scales

Kerboodle: SPAG interactives

Kerboodle: Grammar Reference Guide

Key for Kerboodle LRA resources   Worksheet   Interactive activity

Student Book answers

Below are the answers to any largely non-subjective Student Book activities contained within this unit.

Lesson 2

1 Answers should include the colours red, grey, black, purple for Coketown. Countryside colours are likely to include blue, green, yellow, brown.

2 The metaphor is about 'serpents'. The simile refers to an elephant.

3 The sounds are 'rattling', the references to 'trembling' and the 'piston of the steam engine' suggest rhythmic pounding and booming.

4 Students should show in detail how the repetition of words and structure reinforces the repetition in people's daily lives.

Lesson 3

1 Answers will vary but most should show awareness of the positive associations that most people have with John Lennon.

2 Students should identify the effect of the individual devices, showing how they grab attention, provide visual variety and convey strong succinct messages in an accessible way.

3 The literal meaning of vision is linked to the metaphorical awareness of the wider world.

4 James Chen is founder of Adlens and Vision for a Nation Foundation.

Lesson 4

2 Specifications will be tailored to students' individual items of choice, but all should be written in Standard English, using precise language and include some of the grammatical features in the annotated example.

Lesson 5

The outcome to the activities in this lesson will depend on students' own choices. Ensure that their presentations include some reference to attitudes to technology, as well as factual recount.

Unit 5: Campaign for a Cause

Unit overview

Why are we teaching this?

This unit explores the roles within and texts produced by **a variety of charities**, in order to address the question: 'How can you make someone care about a cause?' In doing so, it develops students' close analysis of **non-fiction writing**, including structural, presentational and language features. As well as analysing, comparing and evaluating charity campaign materials, students also craft a selection of non-fiction texts – employing a range of **linguistic and rhetorical techniques** to inform or persuade their audience.

Students also consider the value of **voluntary work** and the positive impact that charities have on people's lives – helping them to develop a **social conscience** – and are encouraged to focus on a cause they feel strongly about (leading to further **independent research** and consideration of the reliability of information and the possible influence of bias). There is scope for cross-curricular links between the **ethical and cultural issues** discussed and subjects such as Geography or Citizenship. The work of existing charities provides an authentic context for students' learning, so that they recognize the value of becoming skilled communicators within the real world.

What are the learning aims?

By the end of the unit, students will be able to:

- understand the key roles and skills of people who work for charities
- use listening and questioning skills to make relevant contributions to discussions
- identify reliable factual information from a variety of sources during research
- analyse how specific choices and combinations of structural and presentational devices create particular effects
- explore rhetorical features and their effects
- use a range of language, structural and presentational features to persuade readers to support a cause.

How will this be assessed?

Key assessment task	Focus for assessment
Student Book: Writing a report, press release or speech to persuade an entrepreneur to make a £5,000 donation to a charity of the student's choice.	- Employing a range of structural, presentational and language techniques for informative and persuasive effect. - Writing appropriately and accurately, deploying an appropriately formal register.
Kerboodle: Reading and evaluating campaign materials from two different charities.	- Reading critically to evaluate a text's effectiveness, making critical comparisons across text. - Use textual evidence to support points. - Commenting on the writers' use of structural, presentational and language devices.

The end-of-unit assessment on Kerboodle can be used either instead of or in addition to the Student Book end-of-unit assessment.

Note that short Progress Checks also feature in this unit, providing formative assessment opportunities to support students' learning.

Lesson sequence

This is a suggested lesson sequence, but you might choose to alter or add to it to suit your particular teaching needs.

Introducing the unit

1 Charity Roles

- Use existing knowledge to list a number of charities, before organizing them into subcategories.
- Respond to the Ignite English interviews featuring Mathew Grainger and Kate Geary.
- Understand the roles and skills of people working for charities.
- Explain which charity job appeals the most and why.

---

2 Agreeing a Cause	**3 Learning to Listen**	**4 Getting Your Facts Straight**
• Make relevant contributions to discussion, supporting others' contributions.	• Use listening and questioning skills to research and develop material.	• Identify reliable factual information from a range of sources.
• Reach an agreement through discussion.	• Write a case study.	• Understand the advantages and reliability of different research sources.
• Differentiate between international, national and local charitable causes.	• Analyse an example case study, including the impact of direct speech.	• Keep a record of research findings in a way that is helpful.
• Plan for and conduct a Charity Committee meeting.	• Act out an interview in role, developing skills of empathy and dramatic presentation.	

5 Reporting on a Cause	**6 The Press Release**	**7 Into the News**
• Explore how meaning is constructed in a formal report.	• Understand how structural, presentational and language devices create effects.	• Compare structural, presentational and language features.
• Understand how to use adverbials.	• Analyse the range of structural, presentational and linguistic features used in press releases.	• Evaluate the effectiveness of a news article.
• Identify the structural and language features of a formal report, including the effect of adverbials, and employ them to write a report presenting the case for supporting a cause.	• Apply understanding of these features and conventions to write a press release.	• Plan a short news article.

8 Fundraising Appeals	**9 Lobbying for Change**	**10 Assessment**
• Explore various persuasive devices used in fundraising appeals.	• Consider the range and overall effect of rhetorical features.	• Student Book: Write an informative or persuasive piece of campaign material – a report, press release or written speech – to persuade an entrepreneur to make a £5,000 donation to a chosen charity.
• Identify and explain the effects of persuasive and presentational devices within a fundraising appeal.	• Compare and evaluate the merits of different lobbying techniques.	
• Apply these techniques to draft a fundraising appeal.	• Use rhetorical devices in a persuasive speech of their own.	• Kerboodle: Read and evaluate campaign materials from two different charities.

Preparing to teach

Refresh your knowledge

You might find it helpful to refer to the following key points when planning your teaching of this unit.

- There are over 180,000 registered charities in the UK. In 2011/2012, £9.3 billion was donated to these charities – with half of all UK adults making a charitable donation.

- UK charities touch the lives of millions of people – from those they help in times of need, to the more than 800,000 paid charity employees. This paid workforce is bolstered by almost 1.5 million volunteers.

- A huge array of roles exists within charities – from those found in any large organization (such as administrative or human resource-related posts) to more-specialized ones (such as Advocacy Officer or Fundraiser). A wide range of skills is required to work in a charity (interpersonal, intellectual, and communicative), making this unit a rich springboard to develop students' literacy and thinking skills.

- Oxfam (Oxford Committee for Famine Relief), founded in 1942, is one of the UK's longest-established and best-known charities. It was founded initially to lobby the UK government to ease the Allied blockade of occupied Europe, so that vital relief could reach civilians. Over the years, its remit has grown to cover suffering caused by war or poverty in any part of the world, and it continues to lobby on issues such as climate change. Oxfam's work includes emergency relief and long-term development work. During 2012/2013, according to its annual report, Oxfam reached 13.5 million people in 54 different countries. The bulk of its 2012/2013 income was generated as follows: 22% from its retail business, 44% from government funding, and 25% from public donations.

- Oxfam demonstrates how one organization can both lobby for major policy changes and also improve the quality of individual people's lives. However, often charities and lobbying groups are distinct from one another:

  - A charity can be defined as an organization that raises money and acts to help those in need.

  - A lobby group is united in its aim to bring about change on a particular issue, by seeking to influence key players (often the government) in order to affect law, policy or practice. For example, Greenpeace lobbies the government and companies such as oil producers on the need for more environmentally sustainable practice.

Links and further reading

- The Oxfam website features a wealth of information and resources, including case studies and materials written specifically for classroom use: www.oxfam.org.uk/

- A wide range of websites for other UK charities are also available, some of which might be of interest to students during their research, such as: Surfers Against Sewage (http://www.sas.org.uk/) and the Royal Society for the Prevention of Cruelty to Animals (http://www.rspca.org.uk/home), which also includes a range of resources for teachers (such as how to create a media campaign).

- For up-to-date research into UK and global charities, you could visit the website of the Charities Aid Foundation: https://www.cafonline.org/

- For local volunteering opportunities aimed specifically at young people aged 14 and over, including a scheme to reward the number of volunteering hours, visit the website of the charity vInspired: http://vinspired.com/

Please note that OUP is not responsible for third-party content. Although all links were correct at the time of publication, the content and location of this material may change.

Planning guidance and teaching tips

Think about how you can make the materials relevant to your students and responsive to their needs. Some suggested approaches to address key areas are provided below.

- This unit allows students to explore and research issues that they feel strongly about. Encourage them to share and discuss these issues – steering them towards those that might help to broaden their understanding of **social, ethical and cultural affairs**.

- Whilst authentic charity campaign materials and related non-fiction texts can be a motivating genre for students to read, some of the extracts in this unit (including the press release and article from a broadsheet newspaper featured in Lessons 6 and 7) could create challenges for **more-reluctant readers**, as well as **EAL** students. Be prepared to work with these students in one-to-one and guided group contexts to support their reading. Consider those strategies you could use to keep their interest and build their reading stamina, such as using quick **comprehension quizzes** to add an element of competition to their reading.

- Students will use a range of reading strategies to help them engage with and respond to the texts in this unit, but a key focus should be on developing their understanding of how **structural, presentational and linguistic devices** combine to create meaning in non-fiction texts. Ensure that students are aware of the distinction between structural devices (relating to how the information is ordered and organized), presentational devices (describing how the information appears on the page), and linguistic devices.

- Use vocabulary banks, writing frames, dictionaries, thesauruses, etc. to provide appropriate **differentiated support** for students' writing. Ensure an appropriate level of challenge for **gifted and talented** students, e.g. by encouraging more-confident readers to explore a wider selection of campaign materials, through charity websites and topical articles in broadsheet newspapers. Confident writers could be prompted to employ a range of more-sophisticated literary and rhetorical devices, such as allusion or irony, to convey their charitable message in a creative and compelling style.

- Give students space to talk about and reflect on their reading. Creating opportunities for them to discuss and share ideas about a text purposefully can help to engage **more-reluctant readers** who may have negative attitudes towards reading.

- Refer to the **Grammar Reference Guide** on Kerboodle for definitions and examples of specific grammatical features covered by this unit. Use the tools available on Kerboodle to explore the impact of specific grammatical features in context, e.g. the use of adverbials within the formal report in Lesson 5.

- The real-life context and purpose of the texts used in this unit, as well as the final end-of-unit assessment, will help to motivate students' writing. However, you could also provide further interest and support by arranging for **representatives from charities** to come into the classroom to offer targeted inspiration and advice.

- Encourage students, working in small groups, to draw on their independent reading and research to produce a **global charity map**, identifying: charitable causes around the world; which charities support them; and even short case studies about people directly affected by the charities' work. This charity map could be displayed in the school library to inspire students' social and cultural consciences. Allow time in the classroom for students to discuss their independent reading and research.

Lesson focus

Why are we teaching this?

This lesson begins by drawing on and reactivating students' prior knowledge of the charity sector (through asking them to list charities and organize them into subcategories). In order to establish the real-world focus of the unit, students then examine key roles within a charity and the skills required to fulfil them. This provides a foundation for later activities, where students will adopt a number of these roles in order to create a range of non-fiction campaign materials.

What are students learning?

Students will be able to:

- understand the roles and skills of people working for charities.

How you could teach this

A variety of activities and approaches are provided on the right for you to select from and adapt to meet the needs of your students. The Kerboodle lesson player sequence is derived from these suggestions, to act as a starting point for your lesson.

Answers

Answers to Student Book activities, where relevant, can be found on page 131.

Teaching suggestions

Ignition

Ignite English interview

You might like to play Ignite Interview Film 1 to the class. In this film we are introduced to Matthew Grainger and Kate Geary, who work within media and communications for Oxfam, and their thoughts about producing an effective charity campaign.

Resources

Kerboodle: 5 Ignite Interview Matthew Grainger and Kate Geary Film 1

Who or what needs help?

Ask students to list who or what around the world might need our help and why (e.g. other people, endangered animals, rainforests and reefs). Students' suggestions could be labelled on a world map.

Logo a go-go

As an introduction to Activity 1 on page 109 of the Student Book, use the 'Logo a go-go' image gallery on Kerboodle to show students the individual charity logos featured on that page. Discuss the main cause(s) supported by each charity and then ask students to list any other charities they can think of (and the causes they support). You could start students off by suggesting the example of Help for Heroes, which supports injured servicemen and women and their families.

Resources

Student Book 2: Activity 1, page 109

Kerboodle: 5.1 Logo a go-go

Exploration

Grouping guidance

To support differentiation with Activity 2 in the Student Book, issue those students who need it with the 'Grouping guidance' worksheet on Kerboodle, to help them with the appropriate grouping of their suggested charities.

Resources

Student Book 2: Activity 2, page 109

Kerboodle: 5.1 Grouping guidance

Steps to an effective logo

Discuss the charitable logos featured in the Student Book. Ask students to list three rules for creating a memorable logo.

vInspired

The charity vInspired connects young people (aged 14 and over) with volunteering opportunities. Ask students to use the vInspired website below to research volunteering opportunities in their local area. Which possibility most appeals to them and why? This research will help to support Activities 1 and 2 in the Student Book, by providing real-world examples of possible charitable activities that young people could do.

Resources

Student Book 2: Activities 1 and 2, page 110

Weblink: www.vinspired.com

and guidance

Consolidation

Sorting skills

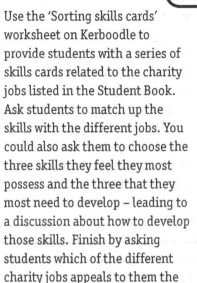

Use the 'Sorting skills cards' worksheet on Kerboodle to provide students with a series of skills cards related to the charity jobs listed in the Student Book. Ask students to match up the skills with the different jobs. You could also ask them to choose the three skills they feel they most possess and the three that they most need to develop – leading to a discussion about how to develop those skills. Finish by asking students which of the different charity jobs appeals to them the most and why.

Resources

Student Book 2: Activities 3–5, page 111

Kerboodle: 5.1 Sorting skills cards

Self-assessing skills

Using the skills cards from the 'Sorting skills cards' worksheet on Kerboodle, ask students to rate their own competence in relation to each skill. You could organize this as a kinaesthetic activity, by holding up or reading out a skills card and asking students to line up along a continuum line according to how strongly they think they possess that particular skill.

Resources

Kerboodle: 5.1 Sorting skills cards

Creating questions

Use the 'Creating interview questions' worksheet on Kerboodle and ask students to write down five possible questions that they think an interviewer might ask a person applying for the charity Media Officer's job advertised on the worksheet. This would be a good opportunity to model and discuss the difference between open and closed questions, and to reflect on which type would be most appropriate to use in an interview situation.

Resources

Kerboodle: 5.1 Creating interview questions

Interview role-play

You could ask students, working in pairs, to adopt the role of either the prospective employee or the interviewer, and to role-play an interview for a job within a charity. They could then rate their own or their partner's interview performance against a list of success criteria which they have devised. If time permits, they could then swap roles.

Researching roots

Ask students to research the histories of a range of charities (such as Oxfam, the Red Cross, and Help for Heroes), which could then lead to a discussion about why charities are set up and by whom.

Ranking skills

Reuse the cards from the 'Sorting skills' Exploration activity. Ask students to choose and rank the top five skills that they think are most required by the charity sector – and to be prepared to explain why during feedback.

Your money or others' lives?

Ask students to discuss the contentious statement: 'It is better to have a career that improves the lives of others than one that earns you lots of money'. Then ask them to stand along a consensus line to indicate how far they agree or disagree with the statement. They should be prepared to explain why they have decided to stand where they have.

Charitable conscience

Ask students to copy and complete the sentence: 'We should all support charities with our time and/or our money because ...'

Extra Time

Ask students to write a job advertisement for one of the charity jobs listed in the Student Book.

Lesson focus

Why are we teaching this?

This lesson is designed to make students think about and choose which charitable causes they most support and why. In order to develop their skills of discussion and debate, they then have to present the cause they feel most strongly about to a group of fellow students, before reaching a consensus about which cause is most deserving of the group's support. During this discussion, students will be allocated a specific role in order to enhance their teamwork and group discussion skills.

What are students learning?

Students will be able to:

- make relevant contributions to discussion, supporting others' contributions
- reach an agreement through discussion.

How you could teach this

A variety of activities and approaches are provided on the right for you to select from and adapt to meet the needs of your students. The Kerboodle lesson player sequence is derived from these suggestions, to act as a starting point for your lesson.

Answers

Answers to Student Book activities, where relevant, can be found on page 131.

Teaching suggestions

Ignition

Local, national or international?

To support Activity 1a in the Student Book, you could use the 'Local, national or international?' worksheet on Kerboodle to help students sort the list of charitable causes. Then ask them to complete Activity 1b by adding other examples of their own.

Resources

Student Book 2: Activities 1a and 1b, pages 112–113

Kerboodle: 5.2 Local, national or international?

Emotive images

Use the 'Emotive images' image gallery on Kerboodle to show students a series of emotive images of people and animals that may need support from different charities. Ask students to identify which cause each image might represent, and also which one moves them the most and why.

Resources

Kerboodle: 5.2 Emotive images

Choose a cause

Ask students to copy and complete the following sentence to explain which charitable cause they feel most strongly about and why, e.g. animal welfare, disadvantaged children, an environmental issue. 'The charitable cause that I feel most strongly about is ... because ...'

Resources

Student Book 2: Activity 1d, page 113

Exploration

Charity begins at home

Ask students to discuss whether they agree or disagree with the statement: 'Charity begins at home'. You could ask them to indicate the strength of their support by holding up five fingers to indicate total agreement or 1 to indicate complete disagreement (or the most appropriate number of fingers in-between). Ask for volunteers to explain and justify their positions.

Constructive or destructive discussions?

In preparation for Activity 4, and as an alternative to Activity 2 in the Student Book, role-play effective or ineffective discussion skills with student volunteers at the front of the classroom. Ask students to use what they have observed to write a list of dos and don'ts for constructive group discussions.

Resources

Student Book 2: Activities 2 and 4, page 113

Ignite English interview

You might like to play Ignite Interview Film 3 to the class, in which Kate Geary discusses the wider skills required for an effective charity campaign.

Resources

Kerboodle: 5 Ignite Interview Kate Geary Film 3

and guidance

Exploration

Ignition

Consolidation

Discussion detectives

During the group discussions (Charity Committee Meetings), ask one student from each group to act as a 'discussion detective' – to listen carefully and observe how effectively all group members contribute (and how well the group reaches a democratic agreement). The discussion detective could then feed back their observations to the group and offer some advice to help individual students to improve their speaking and/or listening skills.

Resources
Student Book 2: Activity 4, page 113

Design a logo

Set students the additional challenge of creating a name and devising a logo for a charity to represent their chosen cause or issue.

Jingle sells

Give students the task of creating a radio advert – with an accompanying jingle – to promote their chosen charity or cause.

TV advert

Ask students to use the 'TV advert storyboard' on Kerboodle to plan a one-minute advert for their chosen charity or cause (to be broadcast on a regional TV channel).

Resources
Kerboodle: 5.2 TV advert storyboard

The merits of minutes

Discuss with the class the importance of keeping accurate minutes during meetings. You could ask the different groups to swap their minutes and compare them in order to identify the main features of effective minutes.

Mini-minutes

Ask students to sum up, in 50 words or less, the main outcome and key decisions arising out of their Charity Committee Meeting.

Relative roles

Discuss with students which of the roles within a formal group discussion they feel is the most crucial in ensuring a successful outcome. They should be prepared to explain their reasoning.

Discussion skills

Ask students to agree with a partner the three most important skills required for effective group discussion.

Talk in context

Working in pairs or small groups, ask students to identify different types of meeting that someone working for a charity might attend – who they might have to meet and why. For example: a meeting between charity executives to discuss strategy; a meeting with local residents to identify problems and ways to overcome them.

Transferable talk

Ask students to identify other careers where the abilities to promote a point of view, listen to others and reach agreement are also essential.

Extra Time

You could ask students to predict and then research the top five UK charities – based on the amount of public donations received last year. Are there any surprises? What reasons can they think of for these?

Lesson focus

Why are we teaching this?

Listening is a crucial skill in many careers – especially so for people who work for charities. Not only does it allow them to understand other people's problems, but it also paves the way for presenting case studies and testimonials that bring a cause to life and encourage others to support it. This lesson allows students to practise their listening skills and then to transform what they hear into a compelling case study.

What are students learning?

Students will be able to:

- use listening and questioning skills to research and develop material
- write a case study.

How you could teach this

A variety of activities and approaches are provided on the right for you to select from and adapt to meet the needs of your students. The Kerboodle lesson player sequence is derived from these suggestions, to act as a starting point for your lesson.

Answers

Answers to Student Book activities, where relevant, can be found on page 131.

Teaching suggestions

Ignition

The importance of listening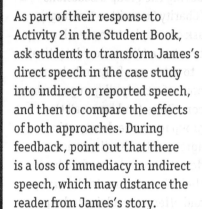

Ask students to discuss why they think listening is such an important skill for charity workers to possess.

As a precursor to Activity 3 in the Student Book, ask students to list two or three ways in which they can tell whether a person is listening to them properly or not.

Resources
Student Book 2: Activity 3, page 115

Silent listening

Show students a clip of a heated discussion on a TV programme or in a film – but with the sound muted. Ask them to guess what is being said and how they were able to work it out. Then play the clip again with the sound turned up and use it to discuss how accurate students' predictions were and why. Encourage students to create a list of non-verbal clues that help to demonstrate a person's emotional state.

What makes people care?

Using the 'What makes people care?' interactive activity on Kerboodle, discuss the effectiveness of different techniques and ask the class to rank them accordingly.

Resources
Kerboodle: 5.3 What makes people care?

Exploration

Direct versus indirect speech

As part of their response to Activity 2 in the Student Book, ask students to transform James's direct speech in the case study into indirect or reported speech, and then to compare the effects of both approaches. During feedback, point out that there is a loss of immediacy in indirect speech, which may distance the reader from James's story.

Resources
Student Book 2: Activity 2, page 115

Role-play rules

Ask students to devise a top five list of rules for creating a convincing character in a role-play. When they feed back their methods (such as key words, shorthand or including pictures as well as words), ask which methods they find most effective and why.

Listening game

As a whole class, play a listening game in which each player has to add an extra item to a list of statements for the next player to recall, recount and add to. For example: 'I like going to the cinema. Recently I have seen … (film title)'. Continue until a player can no longer reel off what they've heard from memory. The last player to be able to do so is the winner.

and guidance

Consolidation

Role-play research

Add stretch to Activity 3 in the Student Book by giving students a topic or issue to research, before asking them to adopt the role of someone affected by this issue and answering questions in character.

Resources
Student Book 2: Activity 3, page 115

Imagining from an image

Show students the image of a Liberian child soldier on Kerboodle and ask them to list and explain the emotions they might feel if they were forced to fight in a conflict at that age.

Resources
Kerboodle: 5.3 Imagining from an image

Case study choices

Ask students to identify the person they would most like to interview and use as the basis for a case study relating to the cause they feel most strongly about and why.

Resources
Student Book 2: Activity 4a, page 115

Creating case studies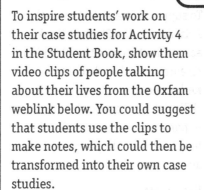

To inspire students' work on their case studies for Activity 4 in the Student Book, show them video clips of people talking about their lives from the Oxfam weblink below. You could suggest that students use the clips to make notes, which could then be transformed into their own case studies.

Resources
Student Book 2: Activity 4, page 115

Weblink: http://www.oxfam.org.uk/education/resources/water-week-learn-resources

Extra Time

Ask students to research further case studies on the Oxfam website about people affected by a range of different factors. Ask them to explain which they find most persuasive and moving.

Listening ladder

Tell students to sketch a five-runged ladder and then ask them to use it to rank the top five ways to be an effective listener – with the most important at the top of the ladder and the least important at the bottom.

The importance of listening – revisited

In the light of their learning in this lesson, ask students to revisit the Ignition activity about the importance of listening and to copy and complete the sentence: 'The ability of its employees to listen effectively is key to the success of any charity because ...'

Progress Check

Ask students to swap their written case studies from Activity 4d in the Student Book with a partner, so that they can assess each other's case studies according to how convincing, empathetic and well written they are. Explain that they should award a mark out of 3 for each of the above headings (with 3 as the highest), before setting a target for improvement. You could use the 'Case study Progress Check' worksheet on Kerboodle to help with this activity.

Resources
Kerboodle: 5.3 Case study Progress Check

Lesson focus

Why are we teaching this?

This lesson focuses on another key role within a charity organization – that of researcher. It requires students to consider the relative merits of different research methods, as well as the possibility of bias and the reliability of sources, in order to encourage them to become more discerning and critical researchers (able to gather relevant and reliable information). These skills will be used later to gather the information required for the end-of-unit assessment.

What are students learning?

Students will be able to:

- identify reliable factual information from a range of sources.

How you could teach this

A variety of activities and approaches are provided on the right for you to select from and adapt to meet the needs of your students. The Kerboodle lesson player sequence is derived from these suggestions, to act as a starting point for your lesson.

Answers

Answers to Student Book activities, where relevant, can be found on page 131.

Teaching suggestions

Ignition

Ranking research skills

To support differentiation with Activity 1 in the Student Book, ask students to use the 'Ranking research skills' worksheet on Kerboodle to sort the research skills listed into an order of importance and then to decide how confident they are that they already possess each one.

Resources

Student Book 2: Activity 1, page 116

Kerboodle: 5.4 Ranking research skills

Revising research methods

Ask students, working individually, to list all types of sources they might use during research, e.g. the Internet, newspapers. You could then ask them to rank them according to how regularly they use them and why.

The role of research

Tell students to imagine that they are researchers working for Oxfam. Ask them to discuss with a partner what types of information they might need to research.

Exploration

Evaluating sources

To support Activity 2 in the Student Book, use the 'Evaluating sources' worksheet on Kerboodle to help students record their ideas.

Resources

Student Book 2: Activity 2, page 116

Kerboodle: 5.4 Evaluating sources

Basically bias

Display the two statements below and ask students to identify the difference between them:

- The red team outplayed and outclassed the blue team.
- The blue team may have been on disappointing form, but the referee was mostly to blame for their defeat.

As a precursor to Activity 3 in the Student Book, hold a discussion about the role and effect of bias. Ask students to discuss where else in life they might encounter biased viewpoints and why it's important that they are able to identify bias.

Resources

Student Book 2: Activity 3, page 117

and guidance

Consolidation

Rehoming research

To support differentiation, or if online research materials are restricted, students could instead use the 'Rehoming research' worksheet on Kerboodle, which contains a series of sources about rehoming dogs. Allow them to base their responses to Activities 4 and 5 on these sources instead.

Resources

Student Book 2: Activities 4 and 5, page 117

Kerboodle: 5.4 Rehoming research

Bias or no bias?

Use the 'Bias or no bias?' worksheet on Kerboodle to encourage students to identify possible bias within their own or the rehoming dogs source materials.

Resources

Kerboodle: 5.4 Bias or no bias?

Canine calculations

This activity provides an opportunity for some cross-curricular numeracy. Ask students to estimate how many stray dogs exist in the UK. Share the statistics from the above source materials and discuss whether students think the figure for the number of stray dogs is high, and also what ideas they can suggest to reduce it (e.g. by encouraging more rehoming).

Dexter's diary

Give students the opportunity to write creatively and empathetically by asking them to write a diary extract from the perspective of Dexter the dog (featured in the source materials), which recounts his first week with his new owners.

Campaign creation

Ask students to design a logo, slogan and poster for a campaign to promote the cause they have been researching.

Vox pops

Ask students to create a survey of five questions and then to ask at least five people about their viewpoints on their chosen research topic. You could then ask students to consider whether and why the people they interviewed expressed biased views.

A–Z

Ask students to create an A–Z of charity, based on their learning so far. A competitive element could be introduced by running it as a team competition against the clock.

Progress Check

Ask students to revisit the required research skills from Activity 1a, and to rate each one according to how effectively they have used it in this lesson – with 3 being very effectively and 1 being not very effectively at all. They should then record a way of improving the research skill they rated as least effective.

Extra Time

Ask students to show their research findings from this lesson to their classmates in the form of a presentation. However, they are only allowed to use up to 50 words and 10 images to sum up what they have learned.

🔗 Weblink   🖥 Presentation   🖰 Interactive activity

Lesson focus

Why are we teaching this?

This lesson moves to another key role within a charity, by focusing on the role of Advocacy Officer and one of their possible remits – writing reports. It is also designed to refresh and develop students' understanding of a type of text they might choose to produce during the end-of-unit assessment – a formal report. While doing so, they will extend their grammatical appreciation of the use of and effects of adverbials, before applying their understanding to writing their own report.

What are students learning?

Students will be able to:

- explore how meaning is constructed in a formal report
- understand how to use adverbials.

How you could teach this

A variety of activities and approaches are provided on the right for you to select from and adapt to meet the needs of your students. The Kerboodle lesson player sequence is derived from these suggestions, to act as a starting point for your lesson.

Answers

Answers to Student Book activities, where relevant, can be found on page 131.

Teaching suggestions

Ignition

Rules for reports

Support Activity 1 in the Student Book by giving students a list of conventions of formal reports (using the 'Rules for reports' worksheet on Kerboodle) and asking them to sort them into three groups: structural, presentational and linguistic.

Resources

Student Book 2: Activity 1, page 118

Kerboodle: 5.5 Rules for reports

Testing views on testing

Ask students to stand along a continuum line, depending on how far they agree or disagree with using live animals to test each of the following: cosmetics (explain that this was banned in Europe in 2009), paint, and medicines. Ask individual students to explain why they decided to stand where they did.

Register rumpus

Show students the opening sentence of a report written in a colloquial register, e.g. 'This ere report is 2 let u know bout the issue of animal testing.' Ask them to discuss what sort of impression this informal approach might make on the reader, and then ask them to rewrite the sentence in a more appropriate formal register.

Exploration

Structure

You could support Activity 2 in the Student Book by asking students to close their books before you hand out the 'Structuring the report' worksheet on Kerboodle, which presents the Student Book report as a stream of unparagraphed text. Ask students to suggest where the breaks should be, and why, and to supply suitable sub-headings.

Resources

Student Book 2: Activity 2, page 118

Kerboodle: 5.5 Structuring the report

Adverbial answers

Ask students to use the 'Adverbial answers' worksheet on Kerboodle to peer- or self-assess the adverbials identified in response to Activity 3 in the Student Book. You could also ask them to experiment by writing further adverbials to be added to sentences in the report to make them more informative or persuasive. The Grammar Reference Guide and/or specific SPAG interactives on Kerboodle could also be used, if necessary, to strengthen students' understanding about adverbials.

Resources

Student Book 2: Activity 3, page 118

Kerboodle: Adverbial answers

Kerboodle: Grammar Reference Guide (adverbials)

and guidance

Consolidation

The case for testing

The Student Book report presents the case against animal testing. Ask students to research and use counter-arguments to construct a case in favour of animal testing.

Create a case study

To add stretch, ask students to research and write an extra case study about an animal used for testing, which could then be added to the Student Book report. Ask them to consider what effect their case study might have on somebody reading the report.

Writing the report

To support differentiation in Activity 4, use the 'Writing your report' worksheet on Kerboodle to provide students with a framework for their reports. You could suggest that they base their reports on the source materials about rehoming dogs in Lesson 4.

Resources

Student Book 2: Activity 4, page 118

Kerboodle: 5.5 Writing your report

Register rewrite

Issue copies of the 'Register rewrite' worksheet on Kerboodle. Then ask students to rewrite this inappropriately informal report in a more appropriate formal register.

Resources

Kerboodle: 5.5 Register rewrite

An executive summary

Use the 'An executive summary' worksheet on Kerboodle to explain that many formal reports contain an executive summary at the beginning, which concisely explains the report's main points for those who might be too busy to read the whole thing. Ask students to use the worksheet to help them produce executive summaries for their own reports.

Resources

Kerboodle: 5.5 An executive summary

Testing views on testing

Ask students to vote on whether they think all animal testing should be banned or not. Ask for volunteers to explain and justify their opinions.

Revising report writing

Give students one minute to list everything they remember about how to write a really effective report.

Progress Check

Ask students to pair up, swap and evaluate the reports they wrote in response to Activity 4. Explain that they should list the conventions of formal reports that feature in their partner's text, as well as setting them a target for improvement.

Extra Time ⏱

Ask students to use the Surfers against Sewage weblink below to research and write a report about the current state of British beaches and how to preserve them for future generations.

Resources

Weblink: www.sas.org.uk

Lesson focus

Why are we teaching this?

This lesson is designed to introduce students to a type of campaign text that they might not have encountered before, and which they might choose to produce for the end-of-unit assessment – a press release. They will practise the skills of close reading and analysis of the structural, presentational, linguistic and grammatical features of an authentic Oxfam press release. In so doing, not only will they develop their reading skills, but they will also identify conventions of press releases to apply to the writing of their own press releases.

What are students learning?

Students will be able to:

● understand how structural, presentational and language devices create effects.

How you could teach this

A variety of activities and approaches are provided on the right for you to select from and adapt to meet the needs of your students. The Kerboodle lesson player sequence is derived from these suggestions, to act as a starting point for your lesson.

Answers

Answers to Student Book activities, where relevant, can be found on page 131.

Teaching suggestions

Ignition

Chocolate choice

Ask students to tell their neighbour the name of their favourite chocolate bar. However, do they know which country the cocoa beans used to make the chocolate were grown in? As a class, discuss whether we have a moral responsibility to know where our food comes from, and also about any ethical issues that might exist within the production chain.

Press release prediction 1

Tell students that they will be studying a real press release during today's lesson. Ask them:

● which person within a charity might be responsible for writing a press release

● what sort of topic(s) might be covered

● why a charity might produce a press release and to whom it might be sent.

Press release prediction 2

Use the 'Press release image' on Kerboodle to show students the picture that accompanies the press release in the Student Book. Ask them to predict what this press release will be about.

Resources
Kerboodle: 5.6 Press release image

Exploration

Feelings about Fairtrade

Ask students, working individually at first, to decide whether they agree or disagree with the statements about Fairtrade on the 'Feelings about Fairtrade' worksheet on Kerboodle. Then ask them to discuss each statement with a partner and try to reach a consensus. This could also be run as a whole-class activity, with students asked to stand if they agree with a statement and sit down if they disagree.

Resources
Kerboodle: 5.6 Feelings about Fairtrade

Purpose of press releases

To provide stretch, ask students to explain how charity press releases, such as the Oxfam example in the Student Book, could be viewed as persuasive as well as informative – at least implicitly. Who are they trying to persuade and what are they trying to persuade them to do?

Resources
Student Book 2: Activities 1a and 1b, page 120

Ignite English interview

You might like to play Ignite Interview Film 2 to the class, in which Matthew Grainger discusses the writing and editing skills required for an effective charity campaign.

Resources
Kerboodle: 5 Ignite Interview Matthew Grainger Film 2

and guidance

Consolidation

Active or passive voice?

Use the 'Active or passive voice?' worksheet on Kerboodle and ask students to transform the statements written in the active voice into the passive voice, and vice versa. If required, you could also use the Grammar Reference Guide and/or specific SPAG interactives on Kerboodle to strengthen students' understanding about the active and passive voice.

Resources
Student Book 2: Activity 1d, page 120

Kerboodle: 5.6 Active or passive voice?

Kerboodle: Grammar Reference Guide (active and passive voice)

Understanding Oxfam's advice

To support students' understanding of the Oxfam guidance about writing press releases (on page 123 of the Student Book), ask them to discuss the questions on the Kerboodle worksheet in pairs or small groups and write down their conclusions for class feedback.

Resources
Student Book 2: Activity 3, page 122

Kerboodle: 5.6 Understanding Oxfam's advice

Framework for a press release

To support students' writing of a press release, give them the 'Writing a press release' worksheet on Kerboodle to provide a framework to structure their work.

Resources
Student Book 2: Activity 3, page 122

Kerboodle: 5.6 Writing a press release

TV news

Tell students to imagine that their press release from Activity 3 in the Student Book has been picked up by a local or national news channel. Ask them to script a news item about it as it might appear on a lunchtime bulletin.

Iconic images

Use the 'Iconic images' image gallery on Kerboodle to show students a series of pictures relating to charity causes and crises. Ask them to identify which cause each picture relates to and to explain why each image is so memorable and effective at summing up the key message of the cause.

Resources
Kerboodle: 5.6 Iconic images

A picture speaks 1,000 words ...

Press releases often incorporate images to drive their messages home. Ask students to choose a single image to put across the message of their own press release without the need for any words. You could suggest that they show their image to other students and ask them to predict what the message of the press release might be before they read it.

Evaluating effectiveness

Ask students to vote on which text they find the most effective and engaging – the press release or the news article – and why.

Top five tips

Divide the class up into pairs. Ask one student in each pair to write a list of their top five tips for writing a press release, while their partner produces similar tips for writing a news article. They should then compare tips.

Extra Time

Ask students to try to find examples of other press releases, possibly by searching on the Internet. Ask how they differ from the Oxfam press release.

 Weblink   Presentation   Interactive activity

Lesson focus

Why are we teaching this?

This lesson tracks the development of an Oxfam press release into a broadsheet newspaper article. By doing so, it enables students to consider how audience and purpose influence choices of perspective, structure and language. Students with an interest in, or talent for, writing are likely to find the opportunity to write a newspaper article both challenging and engaging.

What are students learning?

Students will be able to:

- compare structural, presentational and language features.

How you could teach this

A variety of activities and approaches are provided on the right for you to select from and adapt to meet the needs of your students. The Kerboodle lesson player sequence is derived from these suggestions, to act as a starting point for your lesson.

Answers

Answers to Student Book activities, where relevant, can be found on page 131.

Teaching suggestions

Ignition

Unequal treatment

Casually announce to the class that all the boys are going to be allowed a privilege, such as no homework or going to break ten minutes early – simply because they are boys. Wait for the boys' (and girls'!) reactions. Use this introduction to lead into a discussion about gender discrimination – how it's still very much alive in many parts of the world, and what could be done to reduce it.

In the news …

Ask students to discuss why charities such as Oxfam have a media department (to publicize their work and to raise public perceptions about the causes they support). How might publicity help charities to achieve their aims?

Predict the differences

Ask students to predict how a newspaper article and a charity press release about the same topic might differ from each other in terms of content, presentation and language features. They could make their predictions on sticky notes, which could be displayed and then reviewed at the end of the lesson.

Exploration

Probing the article

Use the 'Probing the article' worksheet on Kerboodle (about *The Guardian* article in the Student Book) to provide students with further critical reading and analysis practice.

Resources

Student Book 2: Activity 1, page 124

Kerboodle: 5.7 Probing the article 📄

Venn diagram 🎓

Support Activity 2 in the Student Book by using the 'Venn diagram' worksheet on Kerboodle to illustrate one possible way of comparing the press release and the newspaper article. To support differentiation, you could give students the statements included in the example and ask them to sort them into those that describe the press release, the newspaper article or both. To add stretch, you could ask students to write up the notes in their Venn diagram in the form of a comparative essay (including quotes from the press release and the article to support their points).

Resources

Student Book 2: Activity 2, page 124

Kerboodle: 5.7 Venn diagram 📄

and guidance

Consolidation

Evaluating effectiveness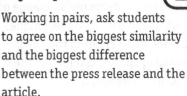

Ask students to respond to Activity 3 by voting on how persuasive they found the newspaper article to be. They could do this by holding up their fingers – with 3 being very persuasive, 2 quite persuasive and 1 not persuasive at all. You could then ask individual students to explain their rating and what ideas they have to make the newspaper article more persuasive.

Resources
Student Book 2: Activity 3, page 124

Framing the newspaper article

Support differentiation in Activity 4 by making the 'Planning template' worksheet on Kerboodle available to students as they plan their newspaper articles.

Resources
Student Book 2: Activity 4, page 124

Kerboodle: 5.7 Planning template

Equality education

Tell students to imagine that they are Oxfam Education Officers. Then ask them to turn the press release and article from Lessons 6 and 7 into a PowerPoint presentation to teach Year 7 students about inequality in chocolate production.

A day in the life

You could ask students to begin this activity by writing a diary entry that describes a typical working day for a woman who farms cocoa in a country mentioned in the Student Book article. Then you could ask them to write a parallel diary entry for a female executive working for a major chocolate manufacturer in the UK.

Key comparisons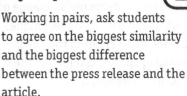

Working in pairs, ask students to agree on the biggest similarity and the biggest difference between the press release and the article.

Chocolate choice

Ask students to discuss how far they agree or disagree with the statement: 'We should all stop buying and eating chocolate until we are sure that every person involved in its production is treated fairly and with respect.'

Equality

Ask students to complete the sentence: 'Everyone should buy Fairtrade products because …'

Extra Time

Ask students to write their news article in full, researching a suitable image and including a caption. Alternatively, you could ask them to write a letter to a major chocolate manufacturer, such as Cadburys or Nestle, persuading them to treat women who are involved in chocolate production fairly and equally.

🔗 Weblink   🖥 Presentation   🖱 Interactive activity

Lesson focus

Why are we teaching this?

This lesson is designed to help students appreciate another key element of any successful charity organization – fundraising – and how language is used to persuade people to donate both time and money. Students revise a range of rhetorical and persuasive techniques to include when creating their own fundraising appeal, and later in the end-of-unit assessment.

What are students learning?

Students will be able to:

- explore various persuasive devices used in fundraising appeals.

How you could teach this

A variety of activities and approaches are provided on the right for you to select from and adapt to meet the needs of your students. The Kerboodle lesson player sequence is derived from these suggestions, to act as a starting point for your lesson.

Teaching suggestions

Ignition

Name that technique

Show students the campaign poster on Kerboodle and ask them to discuss who its target audience might be and what techniques it uses to try to persuade that target audience to support its cause.

Resources
Kerboodle: 5.8 Name that technique

Pocket-money persuasion

In order to reactivate prior knowledge of persuasive techniques, ask students to write a short speech to persuade their parents to double their weekly allowance. Have them deliver it to a partner who must listen and list the persuasive techniques being used. Feed back as a class to create a bank of persuasive techniques to be compared with those used in the Student Book advert.

The Guardian glossary

Ask students to begin by listing all of the words from the Student Book article that they don't know (excluding proper nouns). Then, working in groups, they have to write definitions of as many of the words as they can – before they consult a dictionary.

Exploration

Matching activity

To support differentiation in Activity 1, you could ask students to complete the 'Persuasive techniques matching activity' worksheet on Kerboodle, in which they match the persuasive technique with its definition, an example from the Student Book advert and an explanation of how the technique might work.

Resources
Student Book 2: Activity 1, page 126

Kerboodle: 5.8 Persuasive techniques matching activity

Persuasive presentation

Support Activity 2 in the Student Book by telling students that they are only allowed to keep the two most persuasive presentational features of the Student Book advert (e.g. the image, different font types or sizes, use of colour). Ask them to discuss and agree with a partner the two devices they would keep – and to be prepared to explain why.

Resources
Student Book 2: Activity 2, page 127

Answers

Answers to Student Book activities, where relevant, can be found on page 131.

and guidance

Consolidation

Ideal audience

In support of Activity 3 in the Student Book, tell students to create a profile of the ideal target audience for their example charity advert – in terms of age, gender, family background, and interests. Then ask them to compare their profiles and discuss why identifying a specific target audience is crucial to the success of any fundraising campaign.

Resources
Student Book 2: Activity 3, page 127

Fair pay or no way?

On 6 August 2013, *The Telegraph* newspaper published a report into the salaries of charity executives, in which it criticized the growing number who are receiving six-figure pay deals. To add stretch, ask students to read the report on the weblink below and write their own response to consider whether it's right that people who run charities should earn such large salaries.

Resources
Weblink: http://www.telegraph.co.uk/news/politics/10224104/30-charity-chiefs-paid-more-than-100000.html

Reaching out

Charities use a variety of methods to raise funds, e.g. mail shots, sponsored events, collecting donated items and then reselling them. Ask students to list as many methods as they can and to record the advantages and disadvantages of each one.

Billboard

Ask students to create a billboard poster with an emotive image and slogan to accompany their advert for Activity 3.

Radio waves

Give students the task of producing a one-minute advert for their fundraising campaign – to be broadcast on a local radio station.

Persuasive techniques test

Challenge students to list and define as many of the persuasive techniques covered in this lesson as they can.

Please sir, can I head for the door?

Set students, working in pairs, the challenge of using as many persuasive techniques as they can to convince you to let them leave the classroom first at the end of the lesson. The class could tick off the techniques as they are used and then vote for the winning pair – who should be allowed to leave first.

Progress Check

As an alternative to the Progress Check in the Student Book, ask students to complete the 'Advertisement Progress Check' worksheet on Kerboodle as a self-assessment for their fundraising advertisement.

Resources
Kerboodle: 5.8 Advertisement Progress Check

Extra Time

Ask students to collect and analyse a range of charity fundraising materials from newspapers, magazines and the Internet. Which campaign do they find the most persuasive and why?

 Weblink　　 Presentation　　 Interactive activity

Lesson focus

Why are we teaching this?

Lobbying influential players is a key method used by charities to raise the profile of issues and bring about change. This lesson explores a powerful and emotive speech made at the United Nations by Pakistani schoolgirl Malala Yousafzai about the value of and entitlement to an education for every child. Her courage in the face of adversity and oppression will hopefully be an inspiration to students who are only a little younger than she was at the time of her ordeal.

What are students learning?

Students will be able to:

- consider the range and overall effect of rhetorical features.

How you could teach this

A variety of activities and approaches are provided on the right for you to select from and adapt to meet the needs of your students. The Kerboodle lesson player sequence is derived from these suggestions, to act as a starting point for your lesson.

Answers

Answers to Student Book activities, where relevant, can be found on page 131.

Teaching suggestions

Ignition

Children's rights

What rights should any young teenager be entitled to, regardless of where they live in the world? Ask students to produce a mind-map of their own ideas before sharing them with a partner.

Education for some

Tell students that the government has announced that financial cutbacks mean they'll no longer be able to provide a free education for all children. Instead, they've decided that only boys will go to school. Ask the class to discuss whether this is fair or unfair – and why.

Essential education

Ask students to copy and complete the sentence: 'Education is essential to every child, because …'

Exploration

Lobbying methods

To support Activity 1 in the Student Book, the 'Lobbying methods' worksheet on Kerboodle provides a copy of the grid for students to complete.

Resources

Student Book 2: Activity 1, page 128

Kerboodle: 5.9 Lobbying methods

Speech on screen

Support Activities 2a–2e in the Student Book by using the weblink below to play students a video of Malala's speech to the UN. Before playing the video, ask students to close their eyes and just listen to the speech – noting how Malala uses her voice to get her message across. After feedback, play the video again – but this time with the sound muted. Before doing so, ask students to note this time how Malala uses her body to convey her message. Again, take feedback and use it to discuss the use and effect of rhetorical devices when making a speech.

Resources

Student Book 2: Activities 2a–2e, page 129

Weblink: http://www.bbc.co.uk/news/world-asia-23291897

and guidance

Consolidation

Researching Malala

Ask students to conduct their own research into Malala Yousafzai's life story. How was her life in Pakistan similar to or different from their own?

Planning your speech

For differentiation with Activity 3, offer lower-attaining students the template from Kerboodle to help them plan their speeches.

Resources

Student Book 2: Activity 3, page 129

Kerboodle: 5.9 Planning your speech

Persuasive PowerPoint

Invite students to produce a PowerPoint presentation to accompany their speeches – but only allow them to use a maximum of ten images and ten accompanying key words to emphasize their key messages.

Resources

Student Book 2: Activity 3, page 129

Lobbying letter

Ask students to write a letter to a key player, such as an Education Minister, lobbying for the right of every child to have an education.

Tweet it

Explain to the class that social networking sites, like Twitter, are being used increasingly as lobbying battlegrounds by charities and pressure groups. Ask students to produce a series of tweets (of no more than 140 characters) that could be uploaded to promote their own causes.

Declaration of the Rights of the Child

Ask students to research the UN's Declaration of the Rights of the Child. Which rights do they have? Which are the three most important and why?

Delivering the speech

Ask several volunteers to follow up Activity 3 by delivering their two-minute speeches to the class. Ask the audience to identify any persuasive rhetorical devices and effective oral communication techniques used by each speaker, and also to suggest how each speech could have been improved.

Ignite English interview

You might like to play Ignite Interview Film 1 to the class. In this film we are introduced to Kate Geary and her thoughts about producing an effective charity campaign.

Resources

Kerboodle: 5 Ignite Interview Kate Geary Film 1

Most moving

Ask students to select the sentence or phrase in the Student Book extract from Malala's speech that they found most moving. They should then explain why to a partner.

Speech success criteria

Based on Malala's speech, ask students to devise a list of five key ingredients for a persuasive speech.

Progress Check

Ask students to apply the above success criteria to their own speeches – awarding a mark out of 5 for each (with 5 being the highest). They could then set themselves a target for improving the persuasiveness of their speech.

Extra Time

Give students the task of writing a report that compares Malala's speech to the UN with Martin Luther King's famous 'I have a dream' speech (many videos of which can be found on YouTube). Explain that they should focus on: each orator's purpose; the content of the speech; the persuasive techniques they used.

Assessment focus

Why are we assessing this?

Students have completed a unit on charity campaigning. By studying resources relating to a number of causes and related campaign materials, they have had the opportunity to identify and develop the skills required by people employed by charities in a real-life context. This assessment gives them the opportunity to demonstrate the writing skills they have developed by writing either a report, press release or speech that requires them to persuade an entrepreneur to support their chosen cause.

What are students demonstrating?

Students will be able to:

- employ a range of structural, presentational and language techniques to informative and persuasive effect
- write appropriately and accurately, using an appropriate formal register.

How to deliver the assessment

Suggestions and guidance on how to set up and prepare your students for the assessment are provided as well as possible approaches to marking the assessment.

Alternative/additional assessment

There is an alternative end-of-unit assessment available on Kerboodle. This assessment focuses on reading skills and can be used either in addition to or instead of the Student Book end-of-unit assessment.

Resources
Kerboodle: 5.10 Alternative end-of-unit assessment

Assessment suggestions and guidance

Understanding the assessment

Check that students understand the assessment task and the acceptable formats which they could use for their campaign materials. Emphasize that they are being tested on their writing skills.

Resources
Student Book 2: pages 132–133

Planning

Remind students that they will need to choose an appropriate way to plan their work. They should include this plan as part of their assessment.

Completing the assessment

Remind students to edit and proofread their report, press release or speech. They need to ensure that they have expressed their ideas clearly, appropriately and accurately. Emphasize that they must complete the assessment individually, so that an accurate mark or level can be given.

Timing and writing expectations

Give students approximately two hours and expect between three and four A4 pages.

Marking

You will need to mark this in line with departmental and school marking guidelines. If you wish, you could use the Ignite English marking scales provided on Kerboodle, which will help you to identify specific strengths and areas for improvement in each student's writing skills. This may help you to set development targets as well as build a profile of your class as writers.

Refer to the KS3 National Curriculum and Ignite English mapping grids on pages 154–156 of this Teacher Companion to identify other Ignite English units where these writing skills are covered, or ask students to use the SPAG interactives on Kerboodle to address any areas identified for improvement. The Grammar Reference Guide on Kerboodle contains definitions and additional examples of each of the spelling, punctuation and grammar points covered in the interactives, for your reference.

Resources
Kerboodle: 5 Ignite English marking scales 📄

Kerboodle: SPAG interactives 🖰

Kerboodle: Grammar Reference Guide

Key for Kerboodle LRA resources   📄 Worksheet   🖰 Interactive activity

Student Book answers

Below are the answers to any largely non-subjective Student Book activities contained within this unit.

Lesson 1

3

- Media officer: Works to ensure that the key messages a charity wishes to communicate are publicized clearly, consistently and widely. Writes press releases to raise public awareness of the causes or issues a charity is working on. Sends these to Media contacts, such as editors or journalists, to ensure that they reach as wide an audience as possible.

- Researcher: Researches around a cause or issue. For example, they may work with a Media officer to research the historical or cultural background to an issue. This might involve speaking to those affected, or identifying the most pertinent points from pre-existing documents.

- E-commerce officer: Selling charity merchandise online to raise funds.

- Education officer: Producing educational materials that support children's understanding of a charity and the causes it supports. This role might also involve working directly with teachers and students within the context of a school.

- Fundraiser: Plans and campaigns to raise the funds required to run a charity. This might involve designing mailshots, or organizing sponsored events.

Lesson 2

1a

Local causes: B, F

National causes: D

International causes: A, C, E

Lesson 3

1a The power of education to transform lives, even in the face of great adversity.

2 The use of direct speech creates a sense of greater immediacy and authenticity, allowing a reader to empathize with James and his plight.

3 Ways of showing that you are actively listening might include:

- maintaining constant eye contact
- nodding
- back-channelling (or making sounds such as 'mmm' to show that you are listening)
- asking questions
- recapping the key points made by the people speaking.

Lesson 4

1a The skills required to be a researcher might include:
excellent communication skills, both written and spoken; efficiency and organization; perseverance; teamwork; initiative; a good sense of humour.

3 Basic definitions:

- Bias – adopting an unbalanced or subjective viewpoint.
- Opinion – personal views or thoughts.

Lesson 5

2 In order to make points clear and easy to follow, the report has a clear title, subheadings and a series of bullet-pointed recommendations.

Lesson 8

2 Presentational devices that help to make the text persuasive include:

- an emotive image of a child directly gazing at the reader with a forlorn expression
- subheadings in a bold font to enable the reader to follow the structure of the appeal: from an overview of the charity itself, to who needs help and why, to how a reader can help.
- bullet points to present important information regarding how the reader can help.

Unit 6: Power of Communication

Unit overview

Why are we teaching this?

Students are bombarded with **persuasive texts** and **advertising** in every form of communication they use. Persuasion is a skill that they are developing with their peers and parents in everyday life. In this unit students will explore how persuasion is used in less-familiar contexts. As they are introduced to new topics, they will learn to persuade in **different situations** and for **different purposes**, so that they are prepared for a variety of situations in their working lives and when interacting with the many different forms of media.

What are the learning aims?

By the end of the unit, students will be able to:

- adapt their language and style of writing and speaking for the purpose of persuading and for a given audience
- apply a growing knowledge of vocabulary, grammar and text structure appropriately to their own writing and speaking
- draw on knowledge of literary and rhetorical devices to enhance the impact of their writing and speaking
- draw on their understanding of purpose, audience and context to support their comprehension of a wide range of texts
- understand the term 'debate' and use a range of techniques to develop debating skills
- make critical comparisons of persuasive and presentational devices.

How will this be assessed?

Key assessment task	Focus for assessment
Student Book: Using persuasive devices while taking part in a debate.	• Using persuasive devices to develop an argument in spoken English.
Kerboodle: Writing a persuasive speech to school governors about whether students should be supplied with tablet devices.	• Creating a polished script, drawing on rhetorical devices for persuasive effect. • Structuring the speech effectively, presenting arguments and countering opposing viewpoints. • Using a range of vocabulary, sentence structures and punctuation precisely.

The end-of-unit assessment on Kerboodle can be used either instead of or in addition to the Student Book end-of-unit assessment.

Note that short Progress Checks also feature in this unit, providing formative assessment opportunities to support students' learning.

Lesson sequence

This is a suggested lesson sequence, but you might choose to alter or add to it to suit your particular teaching needs.

Introducing the unit

1 Every Word Counts

- Consider and apply existing knowledge about advertising.
- Respond to the Ignite interview featuring Dominic Gettins.
- Explore how rhetorical devices are used to create particular effects in advertising.
- Analyse mobile phone advertisements and apply this lesson's learning to a related role-play.

---

2 Power of Presentation

- Explore how choices of form, layout and presentation create persuasive effects.
- Compare presentational devices used by two websites.
- Pitch a persuasive website idea for a product.

3 Emotional Appeal

- Develop understanding of how emotive language and other literary devices can be used to persuade.
- Identify and explain the emotive and persuasive devices used in a charity letter.

4 Building an Argument

- Trace the development of a writer's argument in a text.
- Explore how writers can present counter-arguments.
- Write a letter presenting a point of view and a well-developed argument.

---

5 Debating the Issue

- Develop effective debating skills, using a range of techniques to present points of view persuasively.
- Analyse the persuasive techniques used in a speech for a debate on the use of airbrushing in the media.
- Discuss the effectiveness of the speech.

6 A Call to Arms

- Explore the rhetorical and literary devices used to persuade listeners.
- Analyse a speech by Winston Churchill.
- Write a persuasive speech.

7 Talking About Revolution

- Understand the cultural and historical context of a literary text.
- Explore how literary and grammatical features are used for rhetorical effect.
- Analyse Old Major's speech from Orwell's *Animal Farm*.
- Role-play a persuasive response to the speech.

---

8 The Power of Imagery

- Consider the use of imagery and rhetorical devices in a speech from Shakespeare's *Henry V*.
- Read, analyse and discuss the speech.

---

9 Assessment

- Student Book: Use persuasive devices in spoken English in a debate about the use of youth curfews.
- Kerboodle: Write a persuasive speech to school governors about whether students should be supplied with tablet devices.

Preparing to teach

Refresh your knowledge

You might find it helpful to refer to the following key points when planning your teaching of this unit.

- Before teaching, you may wish to refresh your memory or read summaries of *Animal Farm* by George Orwell and *Henry V* by William Shakespeare.

- In the Second World War, Winston Churchill's speeches helped to motivate the Allies and gain America's support. Research Churchill's influence on the direction of the Second World War.

- The art of persuasion has changed and adapted as we have changed and developed our forms of communication. Persuasive devices have developed from spoken to written forms and to all forms of media: print, radio, television, and Internet. The original 'soapbox', where people made speeches literally standing on a box in public, has been replaced by blogs and 'walls', or feeds such as Twitter.

- The original philosophers and historians debated using persuasive devices that we would recognize today. Plato (429–347 BC) used repetition and imagery: 'I've been bitten by something [...] I've been struck and bitten by the words of philosophy.' Confucius (551–479 BC) used contrast, imagery and repetition: 'Extravagance means ostentation, frugality means shabbiness. I would rather be shabby than ostentatious.'

- As paper and printing was developed in the 1300s and 1400s in Europe, persuasion was used more commonly in written form. Religious and persuasive political pamphlets were used extensively in Europe from the 1500s.

- Most novels contain a character who must persuade. In *The Hobbit*, Bilbo Baggins is persuaded to go on a dangerous journey; in *Deathly Hallows*, Harry Potter has to persuade Ron that he has the strength to destroy a Horcrux; in *The Hunger Games*, Katniss gives a short and urgent speech to persuade Peeta that they could die together. Try using a persuasive extract from a recent class novel or the most popular current read.

- The literary heritage contains a wealth of characters who use persuasive words and devices. Dickens's Magwitch attempts to persuade Pip of his compassion when he first reveals himself as Pip's benefactor. In poetry, William Blake uses imagery to challenge presumptions about God. Through Frankenstein's ravings and speeches, Mary Shelley persuades us to consider the possibilities and consequences of science. Jane Austen's Darcy fails to persuade Elizabeth in his frustrating first proposal although he tries nonetheless.

Links and further reading

- Use the following website to allow students to watch some examples of Cambridge Union debates. However, do check the content of each debate for suitability first: http://www.cus.org/connect/debates

- The following online debate about youth curfews could be used alongside the end-of-unit assessment: http://www.debate.org/opinions/do-curfews-keep-teens-out-of-trouble

- Extracts of some of Churchill's most famous wartime speeches can be found on the following website:

http://www.putlearningfirst.com/language/20rhet/chill.html

- Recommended works for students' independent reading: *Churchill: The Power of Words* by Winston S. Churchill and Dr Martin Gilbert; *Churchill: A Study in Greatness* by Geoffrey Best; *Winston Churchill's War Leadership* by Martin Gilbert

Please note that OUP is not responsible for third-party content. Although all links were correct at the time of publication, the content and location of this material may change.

Planning guidance and teaching tips

Think about how you can make the materials relevant to your students and responsive to their needs. Some suggested approaches to address key areas are provided below.

- A variety of approaches and visuals have been used in this unit to support students with lower reading ages and **EAL** students. Explore the visual advertising used throughout students' lives. Link key words with the images and imagery used in the adverts and speeches. Make use of drama and kinaesthetic activities to demonstrate key words, rather than simply explaining them.

- Many of the activities in this unit have been scaffolded using **talk**. Make sure that students get used to working in pairs, which should be changed round regularly to allow students to adapt to working with new people and gain more ideas.

- **Modelling** answers and writing would be particularly beneficial in this unit. Show students how you would approach a task by demonstrating on the board and 'thinking aloud' while modelling it.

- Use the Kerboodle resources to **adapt this unit** to the requirements of your class. Skills-based resources link up with this unit. Select those resources that will develop areas of weakness in students' persuasive skills.

- **Reluctant readers** can be encouraged by the use of film versions and YouTube clips that link up with the texts used in the unit. Suggestions are made in the lesson companions.

- Link this unit to the **'real' world** by emphasizing the use of advertising in everyday life. Encourage students to bring in adverts and discuss advertising used in social media and on the Internet in general. The ability of Internet sites to target advertising at particular users, because of their previous search history, could also be discussed as examples of advertising matched to its audience.

- Encourage students to consider when they have to persuade the people around them. For example, how could persuasive devices help them when shopping?

- Ask students to consider their use of **persuasion in the future**. What would they have to persuade a potential employer to do?

- Remind students that **confidence in speaking** will be part of their future jobs. There is a growing need for students to be able to adapt their speaking to new purposes as jobs change in this increasingly media-dominated world.

- Refer to the **Grammar Reference Guide** on Kerboodle for definitions and exemplars of the specific grammar and punctuation terms covered in this unit, as highlighted by the Literacy Feature icon. Kerboodle also provides **SPAG interactives** to help improve the technical accuracy of students' writing and the application of grammar in context.

- Encourage students to **read for information and pleasure**. Where students show an interest in a text or public speaker explored in this unit, encourage them to do further reading.

Lesson focus

Why are we teaching this?

Students are constantly surrounded by advertising. This lesson will help them to recognize and understand how language is used by advertisers to persuade them and influence their choices. In turn, they will learn how to apply the same techniques to their own speaking and writing, both now and in later life.

What are students learning?

Students will be able to:

- explore how rhetorical devices are used to create particular effects in advertising.

How you could teach this

A variety of activities and approaches are provided on the right for you to select from and adapt to meet the needs of your students. The Kerboodle lesson player sequence is derived from these suggestions, to act as a starting point for your lesson.

Answers

Answers to Student Book activities, where relevant, can be found on page 153.

Teaching suggestions

Ignition

Ignite English interview

You might like to play Ignite Interview Film 1 to the class. In this film we are introduced to Dominic Gettins, head of writing for an advertising agency, and his thoughts about the important role of writing in advertising.

Resources

Kerboodle: 6 Ignite Interview Dominic Gettins Film 1

Exploring advertising

Share your own favourite advert with the class and then ask students to share theirs. Discuss which persuasive techniques these particular adverts use. You could also discuss some current adverts being targeted deliberately at teenagers, by showing examples being used with teenage TV programming and in teenage magazines.

Introducing online advertising

Show some examples of online advertising and slogans and introduce the techniques they use.

Ignite English interview

You might also like to play Ignite Interview Film 2 to the class, in which Dominic Gettins discusses working in advertising.

Resources

Kerboodle: 6 Ignite Interview Dominic Gettins Film 2

Exploration

Slogan generator

Search online for a slogan generator. Then ask students for a noun or adjective and put this into the slogan generator to create random slogans. Discuss whether these slogans are effective or not.

Mnemonic

Use the 'DAFOREST' presentation on Kerboodle to introduce students to a popular mnemonic for remembering persuasive devices. Alternatively, you could use the 'How to make a mnemonic' worksheet on Kerboodle to allow students to make up their own acronym or mnemonic to help them remember persuasive devices.

Resources

Kerboodle: 6.1 DAFOREST

Kerboodle: 6.1 How to make a mnemonic

Slogans and persuasive devices

Before they begin Activity 1 in the Student Book, show students one example of matching the persuasive techniques with the slogans.

Resources

Student Book 2, Activity 1, page 136

  Lesson Player   Image   Video   Worksheet

and guidance

Consolidation

What are the slogans advertising?

In response to Activity 2 in the Student Book, ask students to try to identify what each slogan is advertising. The KitKat slogan is fairly self-explanatory as a starter! You could also bring in some of the relevant products, such as a packet of polos.

Resources
Student Book 2, Activity 2, page 137

Effects created by slogans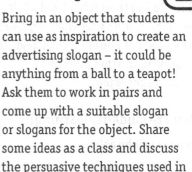

Use Activity 3 in the Student Book to assess formatively what students already know about persuasion, by asking them to explore the effects of each slogan. Share an example with them before they begin. Use the 'Exploring the impact of slogans' worksheet on Kerboodle to differentiate.

Resources
Student Book 2, Activity 3, page 137

Kerboodle: 6.1 Exploring the impact of slogans

Using statistics

Write the statement on the board: 'Two out of three people prefer our chocolate'. Ask students to discuss whether or not this is a persuasive statistic. Discuss as a class and vote on whether it should be used in an advertising campaign.

Mobile phones and persuasive devices

In response to Activity 4 in the Student Book, ask students to look carefully at the four mobile phone adverts on pages 138 and 139. Emphasize that they need to identify the persuasive techniques with the most impact – and also explain why.

Resources
Student Book 2, Activity 4, page 137

Role-play

Ask students to use the role-play in Activity 5 to practise using some of the persuasive techniques they have studied in this lesson. Move around the room, checking which persuasive devices students are using as they complete this task. Support students with possible ways to begin this role-play activity, such as: What are you looking for in a phone? This phone has it all. The best features are …

Resources
Student Book 2, Activity 5, page 137

Extra Time 🕐

Ask students to bring in some examples of adverts with their persuasive techniques labelled. You could then ask them to work in pairs to compare their adverts and decide on the most effective.

Create a slogan 🏠

Bring in an object that students can use as inspiration to create an advertising slogan – it could be anything from a ball to a teapot! Ask them to work in pairs and come up with a suitable slogan or slogans for the object. Share some ideas as a class and discuss the persuasive techniques used in each slogan and their effects.

Vote

Choose and display ten recent advertising slogans from the weblink below. Ask students to work in pairs to rank them from the most to the least effective. Then ask the class to vote on which they think are most and least effective – and to be prepared to justify their opinions.

Resources
Weblink: http://www.adslogans.co.uk/site/pages/slogan-features/new-slogans.php 🔗

Persuasive techniques bingo

Ask students to choose six persuasive techniques from this lesson and write them down in a grid (2x3). Then read out the definition of each technique from the Student Book and ask students to cross out the corresponding persuasive technique in their grid. The winner is the first student to cross out all six of their techniques correctly.

Lesson focus

Why are we teaching this?

This lesson continues the theme of persuasive advertising by looking at the presentational devices used on websites. Students will meet an increasingly large range of text types online during their school and adult lives. This lesson raises their awareness of the power of presentational devices and provides further practise in persuasive speaking.

What are students learning?

Students will be able to:

- explore how choices of form, layout and presentation create persuasive effects.

How you could teach this

A variety of activities and approaches are provided on the right for you to select from and adapt to meet the needs of your students. The Kerboodle lesson player sequence is derived from these suggestions, to act as a starting point for your lesson.

Answers

Answers to Student Book activities, where relevant, can be found on page 153.

Teaching suggestions

Ignition

Colour connotations

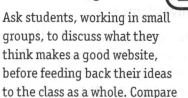

Ask students to think about the colours blue and silver and what associations the two colours hold for them. What do the colours remind them of? If a website used these colours, what do they think it would be selling?

Advertising toys

Bring in some examples of toys for different age groups. Ask students what age they think each toy is aimed at and why. Then ask – if they were designing a website for each toy – which fonts and colours they would use and why.

Exploration

Prior knowledge

Ask students, working in small groups, to discuss what they think makes a good website, before feeding back their ideas to the class as a whole. Compare students' ideas with those on the Kerboodle presentation.

Resources
Kerboodle: 6.2 What makes a good website?

Website design

First locate the relevant YouTube video by searching using the key words: 'How to design a website, Derek Banas on YouTube'. Scroll down his list of YouTube videos to locate the correct one. Then play the first few minutes of the video, which shows how Banas creates a basic sketch before designing a website. Ask students to share what they think are the two most important points the video makes.

Comparing websites

Ask students to compare the two websites on page 141 of the Student Book and respond to Activities 1 and 2. You could use the 'Comparing websites' worksheet on Kerboodle to help lower-attaining students.

Resources
Student Book 2: Activities 1 and 2, page 140

Kerboodle: 6.2 Comparing websites

  Lesson Player Image Video Worksheet

and guidance

Consolidation

Email review

In response to Activity 3 in the Student Book, ask students to write an email to the advertising company giving their decision about which website uses presentational devices most effectively. Emphasize that they should give reasons for their decision, and also remind them that they need to add an email address, the date and a subject (title for the email). They also need to use formal language and paragraphing, because they are addressing a business.

Resources
Student Book 2, Activity 3, page 140

Ignite English interview

You might like to play Ignite Interview Film 1 to the class. In this film we are introduced to Dominic Gettins and his thoughts about the important role of writing in advertising.

Resources
Kerboodle: 6 Ignite Interview Dominic Gettins Film 1

Pitch to an audience

Ask for volunteers to pitch their website to the rest of the class. Vote on the most impressive ideas.

A–Z of presentation

Ask students to list 26 things that would make effective presentational devices for a website – each one beginning with a different letter of the alphabet (for example, a = alliteration, b = bargains, c = competitions, etc.). The winner is the first student to get 23 words out of 26. If necessary, display a copy of the alphabet for the least-able students.

Progress Check: a pitch

As a Progress Check activity, ask students to pitch ideas for a website advertising a product they love. When they have finished their preparation, ask them to pair up and present their pitches to each other. The two partners should comment on how successful each other's websites could be – giving reasons for their answers. Use the 'Progress Check: a pitch' worksheet on Kerboodle to support differentiation.

Resources
Student Book 2, Progress Check, page 140

Kerboodle: 6.2 Progress Check: a pitch

Sketch a website

Using the same product as in the Progress Check pitch, ask students to sketch an outline of their website on plain paper. They could use this during their Progress Check pitch, when explaining their website ideas to their partner. If required, refer back to the Derek Banas YouTube video in the 'Website design' panel.

Extra Time

Ask students to look at other websites aimed at young people. They have to identify what presentational devices these websites use and why.

⌗ Weblink   🖥 Presentation   ◹ Interactive activity   **139**

Lesson focus

Why are we teaching this?

Exploring a charity letter helps students to understand the impact of emotive language and other persuasive devices. This lesson will also help students to understand how to use emotion, anecdotes, first-person pronouns and other persuasive devices in the end-of-unit debate.

What are students learning?

Students will be able to:

- develop understanding of how emotive language and other literary devices can be used to persuade.

How you could teach this

A variety of activities and approaches are provided on the right for you to select from and adapt to meet the needs of your students. The Kerboodle lesson player sequence is derived from these suggestions, to act as a starting point for your lesson.

Answers

Answers to Student Book activities, where relevant, can be found on page 153.

Teaching suggestions

Ignition

Three emotive quotations

Display the 'Emotive quotations' presentation on Kerboodle and ask students, working in pairs, to discuss the three emotive quotations, before deciding which is the most emotive and why. Then ask each pair to join up with another pair to form a small group to compare their answers. Finally, choose students to feed back to the whole class.

Resources

Kerboodle: 6.3 Emotive quotations

Discussing charities

Ask students, working in pairs, to discuss the question: 'If you had a thousand pounds to give to a charity, which would it be and why?' Discuss students' answers as a whole class.

Exploration

Point of view: pronouns

Ask students to read the charity letter on page 143 of the Student Book and respond to Activity 1. The 'First-person pronouns' worksheet on Kerboodle will support their exploration of the first person. You could also decide to make use of the Grammar Reference Guide and/ or use the SPAG interactives on Kerboodle to strengthen students' understanding of pronouns.

Resources

Student Book 2, Activity 1, page 142

Kerboodle: 6.3 First-person pronouns

Kerboodle: Grammar Reference Guide (pronouns)

Anecdotes

Remind students what the term 'anecdote' means. Ask for volunteers to share anecdotes (funny, happy or sad) about their pets.

Emotive language

Support students in finding emotive language and explaining its expected effect in the charity letter, by giving an example before they begin Activities 2a and 2b. For example, 'the huge, frightening, empty world I'd been living in' is emotive because the adjectives draw a vivid picture of how lost and afraid Sammy was.

Resources

Student Book 2, Activities 2a and 2b, page 142

and guidance

Consolidation

Persuasive techniques

You could ask students to complete Activity 3 in the Student Book as a table, using the 'Explaining persuasive techniques' worksheet on Kerboodle. Model an example, particularly for lower-attaining students. The 'Dogs Trust letter' presentation, also on Kerboodle, provides the first paragraph of the Student Book letter for whole-class use/annotation. Lower-attaining students might find it easier to write the emotion created by the quotation, rather than a detailed exploration of each quotation's effect. Ask them what emotion they would expect the reader to feel.

Resources

Student Book 2, Activity 3, page 142

Kerboodle: 6.3 Explaining persuasive techniques

Kerboodle: 6.3 Dogs Trust letter

Snakes need charity too

Ask students to use the Dogs Trust letter as a guide to write a charity letter (or paragraph of a letter) for a less-popular animal, such as a snake. You could then ask them to read their letters/paragraphs to each other and peer assess them by labelling the persuasive devices used and setting a target to use any forgotten persuasive devices.

Blue Cross advert

First locate a Blue Cross TV advert by searching YouTube (using those key words). Play the video clip to the class to familiarize them with it. Then play it a second time, so that students can pick out examples of emotive language being used. Discuss the effect of this language. Ask whether students would give money to support this charity if they could. Why or why not?

Final lines

Ask students to come up with an alternative emotive final line for the Dogs Trust letter in the Student Book. They could write it on a strip of paper that they read out and stick on the wall at the end of the lesson.

Find it first!

Split the class into two teams and ask each team to nominate a representative to come to the front. Then write the names of different persuasive techniques on the board. Explain that you will read out a series of quotations containing persuasive techniques from the Dogs Trust letter. The first student to touch the correct persuasive technique on the board will win a point. Ask for new team members after each technique is found.

Race

Challenge students to write down ten persuasive techniques as quickly as possible and bring their list up to you. The first one to do it wins a prize.

Extra Time

Ask students to consider how the letter in the Student Book tries to appeal to people who love dogs. They should consider the words, the images and the presentation.

🔗 Weblink   🖥 Presentation   🖱 Interactive activity

Lesson focus

Why are we teaching this?

Building and structuring arguments, as well as responding to counter-arguments, are complex skills that need to be practised. Students will use these skills not only in their written schoolwork, but in the wider world. The model letters provided in this lesson, and their analysis, will help students to understand how arguments can be developed persuasively – learning which can then be used in the end-of-unit assessment.

What are students learning?

Students will be able to:

- trace the development of a writer's argument in a text.

How you could teach this

A variety of activities and approaches are provided on the right for you to select from and adapt to meet the needs of your students. The Kerboodle lesson player sequence is derived from these suggestions, to act as a starting point for your lesson.

Teaching suggestions

Ignition

What's the point?

What makes people angry enough to write letters to be published in a newspaper? Bring in and share out some 'Letters to the Editor' pages from local newspapers. Discuss as a class what has made these people angry.

The power of advertising

Ask students to list things that they have been bought or given in the last month. Discuss which of these things they got because of an advert they had seen.

Target audience

Discuss the extracts in the 'Target audience' interactive activity on Kerboodle and then link them to the likely target audience.

Resources
Kerboodle: 6.4 Target audience

Exploration

Letters to the Editor

As a class, look at a letter to the Editor of a national newspaper on the interactive board (using the weblink below). Ask students to come up and label emotive language, facts, evidence, arguments and connectives. Also point out any counter-arguments being used.

Resources
Weblink: the letters page on www.telegraph.co.uk

Reading activities

Ask students to work through Activities 1–4 in the Student Book, which examine the ways in which Jonathan Kent develops his argument. Use the presentation version of the letter, provided on Kerboodle, to support students by annotating it in front of the class when necessary. Pair work will support lower-attaining students. You could also use the 'Persuasive pronouns: we' worksheet on Kerboodle to support Activity 2.

Resources
Student Book 2, Activities 1–4, page 144

Kerboodle: 6.4 Jonathan Kent's letter

Kerboodle: 6.4 Persuasive pronouns: we

Answers

Answers to Student Book activities, where relevant, can be found on page 153.

and guidance

Consolidation

Discussion

In response to Activity 5 in the Student Book, ask students to consider what they think personally about advertising aimed at children. Give them the following questions to scaffold or extend their discussions: What have you bought or been given because of an advert? When have you pestered your parents for gifts? What unhealthy or inappropriate products are advertised to children?

Resources
Student Book 2, Activity 5, page 144

Counter-arguments

Revise or explain counter-arguments before students respond to Activities 6a–6c in the Student Book. You could demonstrate counter-arguments by asking students, working in pairs, to produce arguments or views about the statement: 'School children should never eat chips'. After pairs have fed back their ideas to the class, you could then demonstrate how to use opposing views to produce counter-arguments to develop the strength of students' positions.

Resources
Student Book 2, Activities 6a–6c, page 146

Writing to the Editor

In response to Activity 7 in the Student Book, ask students to write a letter to the Editor of the *Daily Telegraph* presenting their own point of view. To support lower-attaining students, ask them to use the first words from sentences in the letter that most closely match their point of view. Use the 'Letter Progress Check' worksheet on Kerboodle to check that students are using the persuasive devices, anecdotes and arguments they have learned about so far.

Resources
Student Book 2, Activity 7, page 146

Kerboodle: 6.4 Letter Progress Check

Extra Time

Ask students to find examples of adverts aimed at young children. They should then redraft their letter from Activity 7, using these adverts as evidence to support or counter their point of view.

Counter my argument!

Divide students into pairs and ask each student to choose either a 'for' or 'against' position that they have to support in the following discussions. Then write a list of controversial statements on the board, such as:

- Aliens exist.
- Television is bad for you.
- Walking is better than driving.

Explain that students have to take turns arguing for or against each statement, depending on the position they agreed to take at the beginning. They win a point if they are the last person to give a persuasive point. Begin by modelling this activity with two students at the front of the class, to demonstrate what is required.

Agree, disagree, not sure

Ask students to move about the room and stand in one of the labelled areas, depending on whether they agree, disagree or are not sure about each of the statements below:

- Adverts for children should be banned.
- Children ignore advertising.
- Advertising to children puts too much pressure on parents.

Race

Challenge students to be the first one to bring a list of ten arguments for or against advertising to young children to the front of the class?

  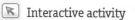

Lesson focus

Why are we teaching this?

It is important that students can present their point of view in a formal debate. This skill will also, of course, be hugely relevant whenever they want to argue a case in their domestic, social or professional lives. This lesson is directly linked to the spoken debate assessment at the end of this unit. It also challenges negative perceptions of body image.

What are students learning?

Students will be able to:

- develop effective debating skills, using a range of techniques to present points of view persuasively.

How you could teach this

A variety of activities and approaches are provided on the right for you to select from and adapt to meet the needs of your students. The Kerboodle lesson player sequence is derived from these suggestions, to act as a starting point for your lesson.

Answers

Answers to Student Book activities, where relevant, can be found on page 153.

Teaching suggestions

Ignition

What do you know about debating?

Display the 'Three debates' image gallery on Kerboodle. Ask students what the three pictures have in common (all are formal debates). Then ask where they are taking place and what students can learn about debating from them. Brainstorm what students already know about debating.

Resources
Kerboodle: 6.5 Three debates

Dove

First use the key words 'dove evolution' to search YouTube for a video of a female model being transformed in 60 seconds. Then play the video, which is a good example of how airbrushing and cosmetics are used to manipulate images for advertising. (There is also a clip of a male model, which is only appropriate for older students.) Ask students for brief responses after they have viewed the video.

Exploration

Picture it!

Bring in some magazines and ask students which images within them might have been manipulated or airbrushed. Ask them to pair up and explain to their partner what makes them believe their chosen picture might have been changed.

Celebrities and advertising

Show students images from the Internet of Marilyn Monroe and Cindy Crawford (both mentioned in Jo Swinson's speech) looking a 'traditional' size and shape. Ask students to discuss whether they think these celebrities look (a) healthy and (b) beautiful. Then ask which current celebrities they think look (a) healthy and (b) beautiful. Finally, ask which celebrities students would use in an advertising campaign for moisturiser and why.

Discussion

As a prelude to reading the speech on page 149 of the Student Book, ask students, working in pairs, to discuss airbrushing. The bullet point questions in Activity 1 will help to structure their discussion. The video clip in the 'Dove' Ignition activity may also be useful, either before or after the discussion.

Resources
Student Book 2, Activity 1, page 148

Key for Kerboodle LRA resources Lesson Player Image  Video Worksheet

and guidance

Reading activities

After reading Jo Swinson's speech on page 149 of the Student Book, ask students to analyse it using Activities 2–4. You could issue copies of the 'Analysing persuasive devices' worksheet on Kerboodle to help them. You could also provide an example to start them off:

- *Persuasive technique* – Jo Swinson uses a list of three places where you can find airbrushed adverts: 'magazine covers, billboards or newspapers'.

- *Effect* – This gives the impression that the audience cannot escape 'impossibly beautiful people', because their images are everywhere.

Resources
Student Book 2, Activities 2–4, page 148

Kerboodle: 6.5 Analysing persuasive devices

Opposing debate

Ask students to imagine that they have to argue against using public money to stop the use of 'impossibly beautiful people' in the media, which can affect people's self-esteem. Their task is to write the opening of a speech against this use of public money. Use the 'Opposing debates' worksheet on Kerboodle to support differentiation.

Resources
Kerboodle: 6.5 Opposing debates

Challenge to negative body image

Develop students' understanding about this topic by showing them the film on negative body image from the weblink below. Ask them whether they think the film supports Jo Swinson's argument. Then ask them to write an extra paragraph for inclusion in Jo Swinson's speech, using evidence from the film and other persuasive devices.

Resources
Weblink:
http://www.fastcocreate.
com/1682823/the-story-behind-
doves-mega-viral-real-beauty-
sketches-campaign

Agree, disagree, not sure

After they have read Jo Swinson's speech, ask students (working individually) to use the 'Agree, disagree, not sure' worksheet on Kerboodle to decide whether they agree with each of the statements or not. You could then ask students to compare their answers with a partner and discuss any differences. Can they convince their partner to change their opinion on any of the statements? Finally, you could review differences in students' opinions and whether anyone was successful in changing a point of view.

Resources
Kerboodle: 6.5 Rhetorical device

Consolidation

Developing opinions

Ask students to use a visual image (e.g. graph, picture or diagram) to show how their opinions about the use of models in magazines have changed during this lesson.

Campaign slogan

Tell students to imagine that they are starting a campaign against airbrushing, beginning with a debate in the school hall. Their task is to design a slogan that uses a persuasive device to advertise this debate. You could then choose three slogans to be voted on for the final advert.

Debate: Beat the teacher

Hold a debate where you present arguments in favour of using airbrushing and students have to present arguments against it. It could be organized so that you make one point and then choose a student to respond. Taking it in turns, either you or the class will win – depending on who runs out of ideas first.

Extra Time

Ask students to design a leaflet informing people about the use of manipulated pictures in magazines and advertising.

Lesson focus

Why are we teaching this?

Famous political speeches have inspired many people to take action and fight against injustice. Churchill's speech quoted in the Student Book builds on the persuasive and rhetorical devices already explored in this unit, and gives students an opportunity to explore a more-challenging and historical text.

What are students learning?

Students will be able to:

- explore the rhetorical and literary devices used to persuade listeners.

How you could teach this

A variety of activities and approaches are provided on the right for you to select from and adapt to meet the needs of your students. The Kerboodle lesson player sequence is derived from these suggestions, to act as a starting point for your lesson.

Answers

Answers to Student Book activities, where relevant, can be found on page 153.

Teaching suggestions

Ignition

The Second World War

Ask students to list as many facts as they can about the Second World War. Then ask them to put a star next to the three most interesting facts. Use this as a basis to check how much they already know and to clarify any misunderstandings.

Invasion threat

Ask students, working in pairs, to use the 'Invasion threat' image on Kerboodle to discuss why Britain was so afraid of being invaded by Germany in 1940. You could offer some guidance by asking them to consider: the distance between France and Britain; how an invading army might travel between the two countries; how long it might have taken. You may need to remind them that Germany would have invaded from occupied France.

Resources
Kerboodle: 6.6 Invasion threat

Rhetorical devices

Use the 'Rhetorical devices' interactive activity on Kerboodle to test students' understanding of various persuasive techniques.

Resources
Kerboodle: 6.6 Rhetorical devices

Exploration

Listening to Churchill

After students have read Churchill's speech on page 151 of the Student Book, play an audio version of the speech from YouTube (using the key words 'We shall fight them on the beaches' to find the correct speech). Then ask students to read the speech in the Student Book again. Finally, ask a volunteer to read the speech out loud in an authoritative, determined and confident tone!

Churchill's purpose

Ask students to work in pairs to discuss and decide on their answers to Activities 1 and 2 in the Student Book.

Resources
Student Book 2, Activities 1–2, page 150

Verbs and pronouns SPAG

Tell students that, for Activities 3a and 3b in the Student Book, they will have to consider why Churchill used certain words. Briefly revise examples of verbs and pronouns with the class before they complete these activities. You could also use the Grammar Reference Guide and/or specific SPAG interactives on Kerboodle to strengthen students' knowledge and understanding about verbs and pronouns.

Resources
Student Book 2, Activities 3a and 3b, page 150

Kerboodle: Grammar Reference Guide (verbs and pronouns)

  Key for Kerboodle LRA resources   Lesson Player   Image   Video   Worksheet

and guidance

Consolidation

Sentence structures

Use the 'Revising sentence structures' presentation on Kerboodle to revise briefly different types of sentences (simple, complex, lists). Then, before students complete Activity 4 in the Student Book, discuss the impact of using lists in a persuasive speech.

Resources
Student Book 2, Activity 4, page 150

Kerboodle: 6.6 Revising sentence structures

Churchill or Obama?

Ask students to use the weblink below to compare the persuasive devices used in Churchill's Student Book speech with Barack Obama's first speech as US President. Students should consider which speech is the most persuasive, giving reasons and examples in their answer.

Resources
Weblink:
http://news.bbc.co.uk/1/hi/world/americas/obama_inauguration/7840646.stm

Rapid research

Ask students to research more about Winston Churchill during the Second World War. Give them a time limit and tell them that they will be asked for their most interesting fact when the time is up.

Comparing speeches

Ask students to compare a clip from the BBC3 Free Speech website (see the weblink below) with Winston Churchill's speech in the Student Book. Ask which persuasive devices are being used in the BBC clip and which speech students think is the most persuasive. Why?

Resources
Weblink: http://www.bbc.co.uk/programmes/b01s4sk3

Fight for a cause

In response to Activity 5 in the Student Book, ask students to write a speech to persuade others to fight for a cause. The Student Book gives the example of a football manager's talk to a team. However, students could choose another topic, such as persuading other students to put on fundraising events for a charity, or persuading local councillors to fund a new youth club. You could also use the 'Fight for a cause' worksheet on Kerboodle to help lower-attaining students to plan and structure their speeches.

Resources
Student Book 2, Activity 5, page 150

Kerboodle: 6.6 Fight for a cause

Post or tweet

Ask students to reduce everything they have learned in this lesson to a 140-character post or tweet, showing the devices Churchill used to make his speeches so powerful.

Mini debate

Ask students, working in pairs, to discuss and decide on the most important thing that helped to make Churchill such a powerful speaker. Choose pairs to feed back to the rest of the class.

Give a title

Ask students to give Churchill's speech in the Student Book a persuasive title, using one of the devices from this lesson.

Extra Time

Encourage students to read more of Churchill's wartime speeches from the following weblink. They should explore the techniques he used to persuade his listeners.

Resources
Weblink: http://www.winstonchurchill.org/learn/speeches/speeches-of-winston-churchill

---

Lesson focus

Why are we teaching this?

Old Major's famous speech in *Animal Farm* uses many of the persuasive features explored in this unit. Students will use their reading to build on what they have already learned, while exploring an enjoyable heritage text. A role-play activity will develop their skills for the spoken assessment at the end of the unit.

What are students learning?

Students will be able to:

- understand the cultural and historical context of a literary text.
- explore how literary and grammatical features are used for rhetorical effect.

How you could teach this

A variety of activities and approaches are provided on the right for you to select from and adapt to meet the needs of your students. The Kerboodle lesson player sequence is derived from these suggestions, to act as a starting point for your lesson.

Answers

Answers to Student Book activities, where relevant, can be found on page 153.

Teaching suggestions

Ignition

Animal Farm

Students may have seen a film version of *Animal Farm* already, or have some knowledge of the text. If they have, ask them to share what they know and make some notes on the board.

Old Major

Use the 'Old Major' image gallery on Kerboodle to display several images of him. Before they read the text, ask students to describe what impression they get of Old Major's character and personality from these images.

Resources

Kerboodle: 6.7 Old Major 📷

Exploration

Context

Give students a brief outline of *Animal Farm*. Explain that the book uses the allegory of farm animals overthrowing the farmer to explore the way in which the Tsarist government in Russia was overthrown in 1917. Say that the book goes on to explore how the leaders of the revolution then became tyrannical themselves, as George Orwell believed the Russian communist leadership to be.

Production and consumption

Ask students to list all of the things produced on a farm, and then to explain what is done with this produce. Pause for thought: Should hens be allowed to hatch their eggs? Give students 30 seconds to think about this and then feed back. Next consider: Should factory workers be able to afford to buy what they make (e.g. expensive cars), no matter how expensive it is? Give students time to discuss this in pairs and then ask for feedback.

'Talking Turkeys'

Use the 'Talking Turkeys' presentation on Kerboodle to share Benjamin Zephaniah's poem as another example of persuasive text delivered by animals. Ask students which literary devices the poet uses to persuade us not to eat turkeys.

Resources

Kerboodle: 6.7 'Talking Turkeys' 🖥

and guidance

Consolidation

Reading activities

After reading Old Major's speech on page 153, students should respond to Activities 1 and 2 in the Student Book. They could work in pairs if they need more support, particularly with reading or Activity 1. Having completed the other lessons in this unit, students should be able to find persuasive devices in Activity 2 without support.

Resources
Student Book 2, Activities 1 and 2, page 152

Linking paragraphs

Before they complete Activities 3a and 3b in the Student Book, remind students that good persuasive writers create links between paragraphs. Use the 'Linking paragraphs' worksheet on Kerboodle to give lower-attaining students sentence frames for Activity 3b.

Resources
Student Book 2, Activities 3a and 3b, page 152

Kerboodle: 6.7 Linking paragraphs

Role-play

Ask students to imagine that they are animals on the farm who have just heard Old Major's speech. Discuss briefly what hopes and fears they might have following the speech, before asking them to complete Activity 4 in the Student Book. Use the 'Role-play' worksheet on Kerboodle to provide help with their role-plays for those students who need it.

Resources
Student Book 2, Activity 4, page 152

Kerboodle: 6.7 Role-play

Progress Check

Model the way students should check another group's performance by having one group perform in front of the class and picking out three things they did well and two things they could improve. Then ask all groups (including the one which has just performed) to perform to another group and give feedback.

Resources
Student Book 2, Progress Check, page 152

Three things

Ask students to tell the person next to them three things they have learned about why *Animal Farm* was written.

Good speeches

Ask students to summarize, in five words, what makes Old Major's speech a good one.

Add a title

Ask students to add a title to Old Major's speech, using a rhetorical question.

Extra Time

Encourage students to read *Animal Farm*, or find out more about the author George Orwell.

 Weblink 　　　 Presentation 　　　 Interactive activity

Lesson focus

Why are we teaching this?

Shakespeare is a master of creating effective images to persuade an audience. Without many props or much setting, he relied only on words. Students will be able to add another persuasive technique – metaphors – to their repertoire while studying a heritage text.

What are students learning?

Students will be able to:

- consider the use of imagery and rhetorical devices in a speech from Shakespeare's *Henry V*.

How you could teach this

A variety of activities and approaches are provided on the right for you to select from and adapt to meet the needs of your students. The Kerboodle lesson player sequence is derived from these suggestions, to act as a starting point for your lesson.

Teaching suggestions

Ignition

Qualities of a man

Ask half of the class to list the qualities of a good father, and the other half to list the qualities of a good soldier. Compare the lists as a class. Which qualities make a good 'modern' man?

Britain needs you

Ask students to think of persuasive slogans for and against people becoming soldiers. As an example, show the famous Lord Kitchener 'Your country needs you' First World War poster, which can be found online.

Exploration

Listening

Before they read it themselves on page 155 of the Student Book, show students some clips from YouTube of Henry V's speech being performed (using the key words 'once more unto the breach' to find them). Ask students to write down or draw any images that come to mind as they listen. Share these images. Ensure students understand the term 'imagery'.

Reading activities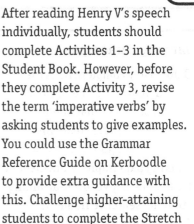

After reading Henry V's speech individually, students should complete Activities 1–3 in the Student Book. However, before they complete Activity 3, revise the term 'imperative verbs' by asking students to give examples. You could use the Grammar Reference Guide on Kerboodle to provide extra guidance with this. Challenge higher-attaining students to complete the Stretch activity in the Student Book.

Resources

Student Book 2, Activities 1–3, page 154

Kerboodle: Grammar Reference Guide (imperative verbs)

Answers

Answers to Student Book activities, where relevant, can be found on page 153.

and guidance

Greyhound or tiger

Divide the class into pairs to explore two key images in Henry V's speech. Use the 'Greyhound or tiger' worksheet on Kerboodle to give one student in each pair a tiger card and the other a greyhound card. Explain that they have to keep describing their animal to each other until their partner guesses the animal correctly. From this, draw out the qualities of each animal.

Resources
Student Book 2, Activity 2, page 154

Kerboodle: 6.8 Greyhound or tiger

Twilight

Use the presentation extract from *Twilight*, provided on Kerboodle, to study persuasive devices in that text and compare them with those in Henry's speech.

Resources
Kerboodle: 6.8 *Twilight* extract

Close analysis

Use the 'Close analysis' worksheet on Kerboodle to challenge students to complete an even more detailed analysis of the speech – looking at imagery, meaning and rhetoric.

Resources
Kerboodle: 6.8 Close analysis

Progress Check

As a Progress Check activity, ask students to practise giving Henry V's speech. Ask them what tone they think should be used to read the speech. Remind them that they can use hand gestures and facial expressions as well – perhaps referring back to the YouTube clips shown earlier. They could work in pairs, giving one suggestion and some praise after each practice. Check that they are able to emphasize certain words and use an appropriate tone to reflect their understanding of the speech. Use the 'Performance peer assessment' worksheet on Kerboodle to check their progress.

Resources
Kerboodle: 6.8 Performance peer assessment

Extra Time

Encourage students to read other famous persuasive speeches from Shakespeare's plays, or to watch them online. They should note down the imagery being used and its effect. A good example would be Shylock's speech in Act 3, Scene 1 of *Merchant of Venice*.

Consolidation

Picture this!

Ask volunteers to come up to the front and draw an image from Henry V's speech on the board. The rest of the class have to guess which quotation is being illustrated.

Match the images

Show the 'Match the images' image gallery on Kerboodle and ask students to match each of the visual images with the correct quotation from Henry V's speech. Give them one minute to match each image with the correct quotation.

Resources
Kerboodle: 6.8 Match the images

Freeze-frame

Ask volunteers to freeze-frame a quotation from the speech. The rest of the class has to guess which quotation they are demonstrating. Alternatively, ask all students to work in pairs to freeze-frame different lines from the speech. Walk around the room guessing which quotations they are showing and giving praise.

 Weblink    Presentation   Interactive activity   **151**

Assessment focus

Why are we assessing this?

Students need to be confident in their use of spoken language for success in both life and work. They have now completed a unit of work that explores examples of different types of persuasive texts. They have also learned to identify and use a variety of persuasive devices. This assessment will show what they have learned by demonstrating their application of persuasive devices in a speech for a debate.

What are students demonstrating?

Students will be able to:

- use persuasive devices in spoken English in a debate.

How to deliver the assessment

Suggestions and guidance on how to set up and prepare your students for the assessment are provided, as well as possible approaches to marking the assessment.

Alternative/additional assessment

There is an alternative end-of-unit assessment available on Kerboodle. This assessment leads to a written outcome and can be used either in addition to or instead of the Student Book end-of-unit assessment.

Resources

Kerboodle: 6.9 Alternative end-of-unit assessment

Assessment suggestions and guidance

Understanding the assessment

Check that students understand the assessment task and have read the instructions and news article carefully. Emphasize that they are being assessed on their spoken English skills. Remind them that they will need to build on what other people say in a debate.

Resources

Student Book 2: pages 156–157

Planning

Remind students to plan their speech using an appropriate format. They should not write out the whole speech word for word, and should avoid a dry reading in which they spend the whole time looking down at their notes. They should write down ideas that include examples of persuasive devices that they could use while speaking.

Rehearsal

Students will need to practise their speeches. This could be completed in pairs or groups, with other students giving positive critical suggestions.

Marking

You will need to mark this in line with departmental and school marking guidelines. If you wish, you could use the Ignite English marking scales provided on Kerboodle, which will help you to identify specific strengths and areas for improvement in each student's speaking skills. This may help you to set development targets as well as build a profile of your class as public speakers.

Refer to the KS3 National Curriculum and Ignite English mapping grids on pages 154–156 of this Teacher Companion to identify other Ignite English units where these speaking skills are covered, or ask students to use the SPAG interactives on Kerboodle to address any areas identified for improvement. The Grammar Reference Guide on Kerboodle contains definitions and additional examples of each of the spelling, punctuation and grammar points covered in the interactives, for your reference.

Resources

Kerboodle: 6 Ignite English marking scales

Kerboodle: SPAG interactives

Kerboodle: Grammar Reference Guide

Ignite English interview

You might like to play Ignite Interview Film 1 to the class. In this film we are introduced to Dominic Gettins and his thoughts about the important role of writing in advertising.

Resources

Kerboodle: 6 Ignite Interview Dominic Gettins Film 1

 Key for Kerboodle LRA resources  Worksheet 🖰 Interactive activity

Student Book answers

Below are the answers to any largely non-subjective Student Book activities contained within this unit.

Lesson 1

1 and **2**

- 'Because you're worth it' – direct address, opinion, exaggeration (L'Oréal)
- 'Melt in your mouth, not in your hands.' – direct address, alliteration (Maltesers)
- 'Leave a man, come back a hero!' – exaggeration (Lynx)
- 'Serious fuel for serious athletes' – repetition, opinion, exaggeration (energy drink)
- 'Buy it. Sell it. Love it.' – rule of three, repetition (Ebay)
- '8 out of 10 owners who expressed a preference said their cat prefers it.' – statistic, fact (Whiskas)
- 'Have a break, have a KitKat.' – repetition, alliteration (KitKat)
- 'The mint with a hole' – fact (Polo mint)

Lesson 3

1 Sammy the dog's point of view is presented.

Lesson 4

1a The writer's opinion is that advertising aimed at children is wrong. He wants an end to advertising aimed at children.

Lesson 6

1 Churchill wants the British people and their allies to work together to succeed against the Nazis no matter how difficult the fight is.

KS3 National Curriculum and *Ignite English* mapping: **Reading**

	National Curriculum: subject content	Unit 1: It's A Mystery	Unit 2: Words of War	Unit 3: Appearance and Reality	Unit 4: Technology Matters	Unit 5: Campaign for a Cause	Unit 6: Power of Communicatio
Develop an appreciation and love of reading and read increasingly challenging material independently	Reading a wide range of fiction and non-fiction, including in particular whole books, short stories, poems and plays with a wide coverage of genres, historical periods, forms and authors. The range will include high-quality works from:	L1, L5	L3	L6	L3, L6	L3, L5, L6, L7, L8, L9	L2, L3, L4, L5, L
	• English literature, both pre-1914 and contemporary, including prose, poetry and drama	L2, L4, L7, L8, L9	L1, L2, L4, L5, L7, L8, L9, L10	L1, L2, L3, L4, L5, L9	L2		L7
	• Shakespeare (two plays)			L7, L8			L8
	• seminal world literature						
	Choosing and reading books independently for challenge, interest and enjoyment	L1					
	Re-reading books encountered earlier to increase familiarity with them and provide a basis for making comparisons						
Understand increasingly challenging texts	Learning new vocabulary, relating it explicitly to known vocabulary and understanding it with the help of context and dictionaries	L1 (TC), L2 (TC), L4 (TC)		L4	L1 (TC), L2 (TC)	L4	
	Making inferences and referring to evidence in the text	L2, L3, L4, L7, L9	L3, L4, L5, L7, L10	L1, L2, L5, L9			L8
	Knowing the purpose, audience for and context of the writing and drawing on this knowledge to support comprehension	L1	L2, L3, L4, L5, L7, L9	L7 (TC)	L2, L3	L3, L5, L6, L7, L8, L9	L1, L2, L3, L4, L
	Checking their understanding to make sure that what they have read makes sense	L2, L3, L5, L9	L4, L5, L7, L8, L9	L1, L2, L3, L4, L7, L8		L3, L7, L9	L4, L5, L7
Read critically	Knowing how language, including figurative language, vocabulary choice, grammar, text structure and organizational features, presents meaning	L2, L3, L4, L7 (TC), L8	L1, L2, L3, L4, L5, L8, L9, L10	L2, L3, L4, L7 (TC), L8, L9	L2, L3	L3, L5, L6, L7, L8, L9	L1, L2, L3, L4, L L6, L7, L8
	Recognizing a range of poetic conventions and understanding how these have been used		L2, L4, L8 L5, L7, L9, L10	L3			L8
	Studying setting, plot and characterization, and the effects of these	L2, L4, L5, L6, L7, L8, L9	L4, L5	L1, L2, L5, L8, L9	L2		
	Understanding how the work of dramatists is communicated effectively through performance and how alternative staging allows for different interpretations of a play			L7, L8			L8 (TC)
	Making critical comparisons across texts		L1 (TC), L5, L10			L7	L1, L2
	Studying a range of authors, including at least two authors in depth each year	L2, L3, L7, L8, L9	L1, L2, L4, L5, L7, L8, L9, L10	L1, L2, L3, L4, L5, L7, L8, L9	L2		L7

KS3 National Curriculum and *Ignite English* mapping: **Writing**

National Curriculum: subject content	Unit 1: It's A Mystery	Unit 2: Words of War	Unit 3: Appearance and Reality	Unit 4: Technology Matters	Unit 5: Campaign for a Cause	Unit 6: Power of Communication
Writing for a wide range of purposes and audiences, including:						
• well-structured formal expository and narrative essays	L3	L10				
• stories, scripts, poetry and other imaginative writing	L2 (TC), L4, L5, L7, L8, L9, L10	L4 (TC), L6, L8, L9	L1 (TC), L4, L5	L6 (TC)	L4 (TC), L6 (TC), L7 (TC)	
• notes and polished scripts for talks and presentations	L4 (TC)			L6, L8	L9, L10	L5 (TC), L6
• a range of other narrative and non-narrative texts, including arguments, and personal and formal letters	L1, L3 (TC), L6 (TC)	L2 (TC), L6 (TC)	L1, L2 (TC), L5 (TC)	L4	L1, L3, L5, L6, L7, L8, L9 (TC), L10	L2, L3, L4
Summarizing and organizing material, and supporting ideas and arguments with any necessary factual detail	L3	L10	L1	L3, L5, L6	L3, L5 (TC), L9	L4
Applying their growing knowledge of vocabulary, grammar and text structure to their writing and selecting the appropriate form	L1 (TC), L4, L7 (TC), L8, L10	L3, L6, L8, L9	L5	L4, L6	L3, L5, L7, L8, L9, L10	L3, L4, L6
Drawing on knowledge of literary and rhetorical devices from their reading and listening to enhance the impact of their writing	L7, L10	L6, L8, L9			L10	L6
Considering how their writing reflects the audiences and purposes for which it was intended	L5 (TC), L6, L10			L4, L6	L8, L10	
Amending the vocabulary, grammar and structure of their writing to improve its coherence and overall effectiveness	L5 (TC), L8, L10	L6		L4, L6	L10	
Paying attention to accurate grammar, punctuation and spelling; applying the spelling patterns and rules set out in English Appendix 1 to the Key Stage 1 and 2 programmes of study for English	L10	L3, L6 (TC)		L6	L10	

KS3 National Curriculum and *Ignite English* mapping: **Grammar and vocabula**

National Curriculum: subject content	Unit 1: It's A Mystery	Unit 2: Words of War	Unit 3: Appearance and Reality	Unit 4: Technology Matters	Unit 5: Campaign for a Cause	Unit 6: Power of Communication
Extending and applying the grammatical knowledge set out in English Appendix 2 to the Key Stage 1 and 2 programmes of study to analyse more challenging texts	L4, L7	L2, L3	L2		L3, L5, L6, L9	L3, L4, L6, L8
Studying the effectiveness and impact of the grammatical features of the texts they read	L4, L7	L2, L3	L2, L9		L3, L5, L6, L8, L9	L1, L3, L4, L6, L7, L8
Drawing on new vocabulary and grammatical constructions from their reading and listening, and using these consciously in their writing and speech to achieve particular effects	L4, L7			L4, L6, L9	L3, L5, L9	L3, L4, L6
Knowing and understanding the differences between spoken and written language, including differences associated with formal and informal registers, and between Standard English and other varieties of English					L3, L5 (TC)	L6
Using Standard English confidently in their own writing and speech	L1, L2	L2, L10	L9	L4, L5, L6, L9	L2, L3, L5, L7, L9, L10	L4, L6, L9
Discussing reading, writing and spoken language with precise and confident use of linguistic and literary terminology	L4, L7, L8	L2, L3, L4, L5, L7, L9	L1, L2, L3	L2	L3, L5, L6	L1, L3, L4, L6, L8

Also available: A wealth of SPAG interactives on Kerboodle LRA 1, 2 and 3.

KS3 National Curriculum and *Ignite English* mapping: **Spoken English**

National Curriculum: subject content	Unit 1: It's A Mystery	Unit 2: Words of War	Unit 3: Appearance and Reality	Unit 4: Technology Matters	Unit 5: Campaign for a Cause	Unit 6: Power of Communication
Using Standard English confidently in a range of formal and informal contexts, including classroom discussion	L1, L3 (TC)		L6, L8 (TC)	L1, L6, L7, L8 (TC)	L1, L2	L4, L5, L9
Giving short speeches and presentations, expressing their own ideas and keeping to the point	L6 (TC)		L6 (TC)	L5, L9	L8 (TC), L9	L6 (TC)
Participating in formal debates and structured discussions, summarizing and/or building on what has been said	L3 (TC)	L1 (TC)		L1, L7	L1, L2	L5 (TC), L9
Improvising, rehearsing and performing play scripts and poetry in order to generate language and discuss language use and meaning, using role and intonation, tone, volume, mood, silence, stillness and action to add impact	L2, L5	L1 (TC), L2 (TC), L4, L7	L1 (TC), L3 (TC), L4 (TC), L6, L7, L8 (TC)			L7, L8